COOKING
the One-Burner Way

COOKING
the One-
Burner
Way

**Everything the Backcountry
Chef Needs to Know**

THIRD EDITION

BUCK TILTON

FALCONGUIDES

GUILFORD, CONNECTICUT
HELENA, MONTANA
AN IMPRINT OF GLOBE PEQUOT PRESS

To buy books in quantity for corporate use
or incentives, call **(800) 962-0973**
or e-mail **premiums@GlobePequot.com.**

FALCONGUIDES®

FalconGuides is an imprint of Globe Pequot Press.
Falcon, FalconGuides, and Outfit Your Mind are registered trademarks of Morris Book Publishing, LLC.

Text design: Libby Kingsbury
Layout: Mary Ballachino
Project editor: Ellen Urban

Illustrations by Marc Bohne

Library of Congress Cataloging-in-Publication Data is available on file.

ISBN 978-0-7627-8211-6

Printed in the United States of America

10 9 8 7 6 5 4 3 2 1

MIX
Paper from
responsible sources
FSC
www.fsc.org
FSC® C005010

*To my mom, Eris Tilton, with great love and deep
appreciation for the many years she fed me,
and to Claudia Pearson, National Outdoor Leadership
School Rations Manager, whose generosity and
food-smartness helped make the third edition better.*

CONTENTS

ACKNOWLEDGMENTS

Books are seldom, if ever, the work of one or even two people. An appeal to friends for their favorite backcountry recipes, and other assistance, brought a food bag of tasty responses. Special thanks go to: Kate Bartlett, Jerri Bell, Margaret Brady, Alexandra Conover, Kitty Ann Cox and Roger Cox, Peter DeJung, Elaine Doll, Tamah Donaldson, Elaine Dube, Melissa Gray, Bethany Grohs and Justin Grohs, Barb Harper, Michael Hock, Ruthe Hubbell, Iretta Hunter, Cliff Jacobson, Lisa Jaeger, Brett LeCompte, Tim Lindhold, J. Scott McGee, Rob Meltzer, Steve Mital, Claudia Pearson, Steve Platz and Shana Tarter, Daniel Robison, James Rosner, Jennifer Rouillard, Ben Sparks, Mark Stivers, Eris Tilton, David Tomco, Ronald Turner, and Woodswomen, Inc.

INTRODUCTION

According to something someone probably once said, a good book passes the test of time. In other words, it still gets read years after it was written. Anything vaguely resembling Shakespeare this is not, but almost twenty years have flown by since the first edition of *Cooking the One-Burner Way* simmered its way into published form. With nearly two decades behind the writing of this third edition, along with the updated and new information and recipes it contains, and the message herein, it continues to reach quite a few novice, intermediate, and even advanced outdoor cooks. I will boldly, therefore, claim that this is a good book.

Whether or not this is your first time within these paper covers, know that you do not hold just another outdoor cookbook in your hands. Sure, it tells you how to cook outdoors, and those of you who are already accomplished at it will be more accomplished by the time you've digested all of this information; however, this cookbook goes beyond a mere collection of recipes and culinary tips for kitchens situated far from a roadhead. It also provides all you need to know about choosing food and stoves and cooking gear; how much of what you'll need for so many days; special considerations, such as high altitude and extreme cold; information about camp hygiene, so you won't consume things you *don't* want in your body; how to leave your campsite environmentally clean; and how to prepare everything from Yippee-Ki-Yay Cowboy Coffee to Wild Currant Cottlestone Pie via your choice of entree. Briefly stated, this book gives you the opportunity to forsake a food-as-fuel attitude and become a backcountry chef.

This book stands firmly on a one-burner backcountry stove foundation. One-burners are readily available, lightweight, compact, and, with many products, infinitely functional. In fact, since the second edition, the greatest changes in backcountry cooking are associated with stoves; they are lighter, faster, and more efficient than ever before. One-burners ease the stress on Mother Earth in wild areas where she has withstood— just barely in many locales—too many open fires in too many places for too long a time. Although campfires are acceptable, or at least tolerated, in some spots, with a one-burner stove you'll be able to dine sooner, and more "elegantly," in regions with limited wood, such as above the tree line, in deserts, and on snow. More and more backcountry chefs need to be taking only pictures and leaving nothing behind.

In this third edition, you'll be introduced to (if you haven't met before) innovative cookware created since the second edition, and to suppliers that did not exist ten years ago. And, yes, there are more than two dozen new recipes, along with all of the old ones.

Sixty-two days in Idaho's Frank Church–River of No Return Wilderness, where a small Cessna dropped resupplies, was my longest personal trip. Numerous one-nighters are represented, by cooking on the tailgate of a Bronco after fishing the beaver ponds along Colorado's Middle Quartz Creek. In between lie over forty years' worth of boiling, baking, poaching, and frying out of backpacks, canoe bags, sea-kayak bags, and saddlebags. A long list of memories includes coaxing hot soup out of cold pots at 18,000 feet in Alaska, swatting mosquitoes while fresh fish sizzled in Florida, melting Wind River Range snow for morning coffee, and dropping just-picked Maine blueberries into a lakeside pudding. The list is far from done.

Over the years, and over a lot of different stoves, my own journey has encompassed solid lumps of scorched mac-and-cheese to fresh-baked bread and delicately seasoned casseroles. This book will make your journey to chef-hood much shorter . . . and far tastier.

Buck Tilton
Lander, Wyoming
Spring 2013

There are lots of great recipes in this book, and some of them are easy to categorize. Take a look at the following key to see some of the recipe types. Then look for the appropriate icon next to the recipe titles to find exactly what you want.

KEY

 Popular Variations on the Theme

 Popular Mixes

 Truly Gourmet

 Truly Something

Pre-Trip Planning

Nutrition: Body Fuel

Food, whatever its taste and psychological benefits, does provide fuel for the human engine. It's go-power, and the worth of the go is called its nutritional value. Nutrition, like politics, ends up being largely a matter of personal opinion, but a shortage of nutrients, despite who you voted for, causes everyone to have energy slumps that bring early fatigue, grumpiness, lassitude, mind numbness, and a predisposition for getting sick. Start every backcountry trip by planning to eat well nutritionally.

ENERGY SOURCES

Your body has three sources of energy: carbohydrates, fats, and, to some extent, proteins. Although all food ends up being digested into simple compounds before it can be burned for power, **carbohydrates** (sugars and starches) digest the quickest and easiest. Simple carbohydrates (simple sugars: table sugar, brown sugar, date sugar, honey, molasses) are small molecular units that break down very fast, entering the bloodstream soon after you eat them. You get an energy boost right away. But most sugars are burned so quickly that energy levels can suddenly fall below your starting point if all you eat is simple carbohydrates. Therefore, complex carbohydrates (strings of simple sugars called starches) need to comprise a major portion of your diet. As a more-complex molecular unit, starches break down more slowly, providing power for the long haul. In the backcountry, generally speaking, carbohydrates should supply about 60 percent of the calories in your diet.

Complex Carbohydrate Sources: Whole grains and whole-grain products (cereals, breads), pasta, fruits, and vegetables.

Fat is necessary for a healthy life . . . but not too much fat. In fact, your body will manufacture fat from carbohydrates and proteins if you run short. Your body worries about running out of fat so much that it'll store unbelievable quantities against a fatless day. Unfortunately (and unhealthily), you don't really know when you have too much of a good thing. Fat breaks down very slowly in the digestive process, so more time is required for it to provide energy. There are saturated fats and unsaturated fats, and most fats, animal and vegetable, are combinations of both kinds. Saturated fats are harder and stick to your arteries better, and so they're considered less healthy than unsaturated fats. Cholesterol (lipoprotein) is a substance found in animal fats. Low-density lipoproteins (LDL) seem to lend themselves to heart disease more than high-density lipoproteins (HDL). HDLs have even been associated with a reduced risk of heart disease. Fats have a devilish quality: They tend to taste really good. But fats should supply only approximately 25 percent of your diet.

Fat Sources: Butter, margarine, oils, cheeses, meats, and nuts.

Proteins are made up of amino acids, and amino acids are the basic substance of human tissue. Proteins are not a primary energy source, but your body will use them if nothing else is available, or if you exercise for a long period of time. But since tissue is continually lost and replaced (and new tissue is built when you exercise), proteins are essential to life. All of the amino acids are synthesized by your body—except for eight, which have to be eaten. A "complete protein" has all eight of these amino acids. Eggs, milk, and meat (including fish) are complete. Other foods, such as grains, seeds, nuts, and legumes, contain incomplete proteins, but since they're incomplete in different ways, some of them can be combined to form complete proteins. Legumes (soybeans, navy beans, kidney beans, pinto beans, lima beans, peanuts, black-eyed peas, chickpeas, split peas, lentils) combine with seeds and nuts to form complete proteins, and milk products and whole grains combine completely also. Most whole grains combine with most legumes to complete the protein package. Some milk products combine with some seeds and nuts to form complete proteins. Proteins need to make up about 15 percent of your diet.

Protein Sources: Meat, milk and milk products, eggs, seeds, nuts, legumes, whole grains.

Boost your protein intake by:

- Combining rice with legumes, wheat, seeds, or milk products. Check out Creamy Rice Pudding (see Desserts, page 148) or Quick Curried Rice (Entrees, page 97).
- Combining wheat with legumes, nuts, seeds, or milk products. Check out Pizza (see Entrees, page 121) or Peanut Butter Bread (Backcountry Baking).
- Combining legumes with corn, seeds, whole grains, or milk products. Check out Essential Falafel (see Entrees, page 118).

- Combining seeds with milk products. Check out Hot or Cold "Szechwan" Noodles (see Entrees, page 108) or Barb's Granola (Breakfasts, page 58).
- Combining potatoes and milk products. Check out Spicy Shepherd's Pie (Entrees, page 115).

VITAMINS, MINERALS, FIBER

You won't function for long without **vitamins,** and these little organic molecules must be eaten. Vitamins are necessary for food to be processed into energy for life. There are thirteen known vitamins. Some are fat-soluble (A, D, E, K) and are stored in fatty tissue and organ tissue of the body. Some are water-soluble (C and the Bs), cannot be stored, and wash out when you sweat or urinate. As long as you eat a balanced diet, you'll probably get the vitamins you need. On extended backcountry trips you may consider taking a daily multivitamin that meets the recommended daily allowances (RDA) of the National Academy of Sciences. To exceed the RDA, especially with fat-soluble vitamins, may be harmful.

Traces of several **minerals** are also required for you to continue to function. These minerals are generally divided into two classes: 1) major minerals (such as calcium) that you need more of than 2) minor minerals (such as iron). Once again, a balanced diet supplies all the minerals you need. If you decide to take supplements, do not exceed the RDA. Remember: Taking vitamin/mineral supplements is like trying to cheat your way to health. They are not a substitute for eating right.

Fiber is that stuff in some foods that you eat but don't digest, yet it plays a vital role in health. There are two kinds of fibers: insoluble (whole-grain products, bran, cellulose) and soluble (oats, oat bran, fruits, vegetables, nuts, beans). Insoluble fiber won't hold much water, so it moves quickly through your digestive tract and encourages other food to move quickly, keeping your bowel movements regular. Too much insoluble fiber may produce too much movement. Soluble fiber absorbs water and becomes gooey, sticking to other foods and slowing their assimilation into your body. This is healthy because soluble fibers stick to some potentially harmful cholesterol better than your body does, so it is carried out.

WATER

Water probably ranks as the most common thing your body needs more of on a backcountry trip. It is the most important nutrient that passes your lips, something you need almost as critically as air, the medium of energy production and body temperature control and waste removal of metabolic by-products. To feel well and perform well, you've got to drink a lot of water, because you lose it constantly through sweat and urination and defecation, even through breathing.

The amount of water a human needs remains a somewhat hotly debated topic. You will be fine, however—in most environments—if you start each day with about a half-liter (16 ounces) of water. During periods of exercise you should be downing about 8 more ounces every fifteen or twenty minutes. For wilderness travel, and for life in general, the old piece of advice to drink enough water to keep your urine clear and copious rings with truth . . . as long as you are also eating regularly.

NUTRITION IN THE COLD OUTDOORS

Although your need for vitamins and minerals does not change in a cold environment, your need for water goes up and your energy requirements are increased. To meet the increased need, you should drink more and eat more. The single most important factor in cold-weather food consumption is carrying food you enjoy eating. The nutrient breakdown should be approximately the same: 60 percent carbohydrate, 25 percent fat, 15 percent protein. Carbohydrate intake is especially important to replenish muscle energy stores in order to prevent excess fatigue, which often leads to cold injury. Cold tolerance may be improved for most people by a high-fat snack (about one-third of the calories from fat) every couple of hours: one or two snacks between breakfast and lunch, another one between lunch and dinner, and one more before crawling into your sleeping bag. If you're one of those people who awaken cold during the night, pack a snack into your sleeping bag. Consider making a water bottle of hot chocolate before bedtime. In the sleeping bag, it provides warmth by contact. Later in the night it provides warmth by calories. (Make sure the top is screwed on tight!)

NUTRITION AT HIGH ALTITUDE

Higher altitudes tend to be cold, and the same cold-weather recommendations apply, with one exception: Fat is not tolerated as well at higher altitudes (above 16,000 feet). Fat tolerances decrease as altitude increases. You will probably function better if you change high-fat snacks to high-energy, high-carbohydrate snacks. There is also some evidence indicating that people on high-carb diets—about 70 percent carbohydrate—acclimatize better to higher altitudes. Because altitude often affects your appetite, it is critical to carry food you crave. Proper nutrition is important, but not as important as an adequate caloric and fluid intake—and not as important as healthy physical conditioning, and proper clothing and gear.

Food and Menu Planning

Whether it's a paddling weekend on the lakes of Minnesota or a month on a high California mountain range, nothing upsets people faster than having too little or rotten-tasting food. Too much can also be a problem, especially if you're required to carry it or pull it, but an overabundance of grub doesn't usually result in hatred of the food packer/cook. So here are some questions to ask yourself and your traveling companions before purchasing and packing the food.

1. How long will you be in the backcountry? For short trips (less than a week), I tend to count the specific meals needed, preplan a menu, and repackage ingredients into a Bag-a-Feast per meal. On longer trips, package your food in bulk bags and plan your menus as you go. Both of these methods will be described in greater detail later in this chapter.

2. What's the time of year and level of expected activity? Cold weather and high-intensity exercise will increase your body's caloric needs. Are you planning to fish or hunt? Fish can be a great supplement to a diet, but if you get skunked you can end up very hungry.

3. Who's going with you? A coed group of preadolescents eats far less than a group of guys in their twenties. Most small folks eat less than most large folks. People experienced with outdoor cooking and travel tend to eat more than novices (instructors versus students). Some people just plain eat more than other people. When packing for groups, this usually evens out somewhere along the line; otherwise, "Practice makes perfect."

4. Does the group have any special needs? Allergies, diabetes, religion, and even likes and dislikes greatly affect what people will eat. An informal (or perhaps formal, in some circumstances) questionnaire is often helpful.

5. How much money do you have? Yes, you must have a certain amount, but by staying away from prepackaged meals and specialty

items, you'll be sure to save dollars as well as cut down on wasteful packaging.

TOTAL RATION PLANNING VERSUS SPECIFIC MENU PLANNING

Basically, you have two options for food and menu planning. You will probably find yourself using them both regularly, but in different situations.

Option 1: Total Ration Planning

Total Ration Planning is your first choice for backcountry food planning. It works just as well for two people on a ten-day Maine coastal kayaking trip as it does for a group of twelve backpackers descending Utah's Grand Gulch.

Total Ration Planning grants you the freedom to pack a wide variety of dried foods, allowing for endless meal options. When you menu-plan as you go, instead of ahead of time, you are allowed to be spontaneous, adapting to the day's preferences and tasks. Food requirements change easily with the weather and your personal tastes.

Also, by cooking from scratch, you minimize prepackaged foods, usually increase nutrition, cut down on fat and salt, get to use your imagination, and, most important, impress your companions with your cooking prowess.

How Do I Do It? Important Details:

Number of days (D): This is an easy one to figure out, and important to future calculations.

Number of people who want to eat (P): Usually everyone wants to eat. Don't trust them if they say they don't. Once they smell your cooking, they'll change their minds.

Caloric needs and weight (W): Some people work these out separately and specifically. I have had a lot of luck generalizing caloric intake, and only nearly starved to death once. If you want to work out your caloric intake specifically, there is a chart in the appendix with the most commonly used backpacking foods and their corresponding calories per pound. And you'll find quite a few online calorie-counting programs, such as a free, detailed program at fitwatch.com.

How Much Food Do I Need?

Food equals weight. And the more energy you exert, the more food you will need. Remember, extreme weather greatly increases your energy output. Below you will find four plans for different types of outdoor adventures. Read through them and pick the one that most closely resembles the trip you are currently planning.

> *Plan 1:* This plan is utilized in very warm conditions when you don't feel super-hungry or when activity level is very low. For example: base camps or water trips where you supplement your diet with fishing and/or some fresh and canned food. Pack 1.5 pounds of food per person per day. Calories will add up to roughly 2,200 to 2,500 per day.

> *Plan 2:* In my opinion, this is the most generally useful approach to packing food. It keeps most folks content with the food supply on the average backcountry excursion, from spring through fall. Pack between 1.75 and 2.0 pounds of food per person per day. Calculated calories should add up to roughly 2,500 to 3,000 per day.

> *Plan 3:* This plan works best for folks who are traveling in cold environments or are putting in extremely heavy workdays. Pack 2.0 to 2.25 pounds of food per person per day. Calculated calories should add up to roughly 3,000 to 3,500 per day.

> *Plan 4:* This plan is utilized in only the most extreme environments: extreme cold, high-altitude mountaineering, Continental Divide through-hikers, and the like. Pack 2.5 pounds of food per person per day, or more. At this level eating becomes a discipline more than a result of hunger.

Here is an example of the formula—PxDxW— at work:

Two average people are taking a ten-day July backpacking and fishing trip in the Rockies. How much food do they need?

Two people (P) x 10 days (D) x 1.75 pounds food/day (W=Plan 2) = 35.0 pounds of food. These two hikers need to pack 35 pounds of food total for their ten-day trip.

What to Bring: Types of Food

If you are inexperienced with backcountry cooking, may I suggest bringing a wide variety of foods and a copy of this book; then, have fun.

Break food rationing down into eight categories and distribute the food as follows:

1. ***Breakfasts:*** About 15 percent of the total weight. Examples: Bagels, Cream of Wheat, Grape-Nuts, granola, hash browns, oatmeal.

2. ***Dinners:*** About 20 percent of the total weight. Examples: Bulgur, couscous, dried potatoes, falafel, lentils, pasta, instant beans, rice, tortillas.

3. ***Flour:*** About 10 percent of total weight. Examples: Wheat, white, cornmeal, baking mix, muffin mix, bread mix.

4. ***High-fat items:*** About 13 percent of total weight. Examples: Cheese, margarine, meats, oil, peanut butter.

5. ***Munchables:*** About 20 percent of total weight. Examples: Candy, crackers, dried fruit, fruit bars, high-energy bars, pita bread, nuts and seeds, trail mix.

6. ***Drinks and sugars:*** About 10 percent of total weight. Examples: Sugar, fruit crystals, honey, hot chocolate, gelatin.

7. ***Desserts:*** About 3 percent of total weight. Examples: Brownie mix, cake mix, cheesecake mix, pudding mix.

8. ***Miscellaneous:*** About 8 percent of total weight. Examples: Milk powder, soup mix, dried vegetables, egg powder, tomato base.

Total Ration Planning is not an exact science. If you add up the percentages in the eight categories, you will see that the grand total equals only 99 percent. This gives you a little freedom in packaging and planning. There is a lot of flexibility with the categories, but it is important that your total weight measures up. If you come up light when you weigh your food bag, throw in a couple of your favorite items. If you come up heavy, get rid of something.

The more you use this method, the more you will learn the ins and outs of the foods that will most please you and your companions. If you are having trouble knowing where to begin, Table A (page 13) will give you a general plan. The table is based on a ten-day ration for two people, so remember to adjust for number of days times the number of people times the number of pounds per day to arrive at your grand total of food needed.

Non- or low-caloric items, although you need to bring them along, should not be counted in your total poundage. Examples of these items include: spices, bouillon cubes, hot sauce, coffee, items with NutraSweet or other artificial sweeteners, small amounts of dried vegetables, and so on.

Once you become more experienced with Total Ration Planning, feel free to substitute your favorite foods into the plan. But be careful to substitute foods of approximately equal caloric value. For example, if you substitute 2 pounds of cheese (3,200 calories) with 2 pounds of tuna (1,400), you will end up significantly reducing your total by 1,800 calories. Additionally, many people decide not to bake in the backcountry. Remember, if you're not going to bring flour, you should consider substituting breads and crackers.

Option 2: Specific Menu Planning

Specific Menu Planning works well on short trips (less than a week), or when you have little time or energy to spend on, or interest in, food preparation in the field. Although it is not required, this is certainly the best plan for high-altitude or extreme cold-weather trips. It's just so convenient when you crawl into camp, exhausted, to have a Bag-a-Feast (see Repackaging and Resupplying, page 15) ready to go. You don't have to think.

How Do I Do It? Important Details:

Number of specific meals: How many breakfasts, lunches, and dinners will you need?

Trip menu: You will need to decide what you will eat at those specific meals.

Number of people: You will need this figure in order to estimate the amount of food needed per meal, and some bulk items (e.g., beverages, dry milk, oil, and so on). As a starting point, somewhere between three-fourths of a pound and 1 pound of dry ingredients per meal usually satisfies about three hungry outdoor types.

Final check: As a final check, always weigh your food to see if you're in the correct weight range for the number of people (P) times number of days (D) times number of pounds per day (W).

Sample Menu for a Weekend Trip:

FRIDAY	SATURDAY
Breakfast	*Breakfast*
Granola and milk	Pancakes and syrup
Dried fruit	Dried fruit
Hot chocolate	International Coffee
Munchables	*Munchables*
Cheese and crackers	Meat and crackers
Fruit bars, gorp	Energy bars and gorp
Fruit drink	Energy drink
Dinner	*Dinner*
Tea	Tea
Curried Rice	Lisagna Lasagna
Fruit Crunch	Pudding

CONSIDERATIONS FOR SPECIAL ENVIRONMENTS

If you're trying to save weight and water, freeze-dried foods can usually cut 20 percent of your total food poundage and save you significant amounts of fuel as well. This can be very helpful in the desert where water is scarce, or in winter when you're melting snow for water.

Some people are willing to go completely freeze-dried, while others will occasionally throw a few such meals in for special situations like those listed above, or when you're high up in the mountains and almost too tired to breathe, never mind cook. Their light weight also means they can serve as ideal extra food rations: Forget them in the bottom of your pack until an emergency arises, then pull them out and just add hot water.

Table A: Sample Food Ration Plan

(Ten-day ration for two people)

TOTAL	1.5 lbs./day per person 30 lbs.	1.75 lbs./day per person 35 lbs.	2 lbs./day per person 40 lbs.	2.25 lbs./day per person 45 lbs.
BREAKFASTS **% OF TOTAL LBS.**	**15%**	**15%**	**15%**	**15%**
Bagels	1.0	1.0	2.0	2.0
Cream of Wheat		0.5	0.5	0.5
Grape-Nuts	1.0	1.0	1.0	1.0
Granola	0.5	0.75	0.5	1.25
Hash browns	1.0	1.0	1.0	1.0
Oatmeal	1.0	1.0	1.0	1.0
Subtotal	**4.5**	**5.25**	**6.0**	**6.75**
DINNERS **% OF TOTAL LBS.**	**20%**	**20%**	**20%**	**15%**
Bulgur	0.5	0.5	0.5	0.5
Couscous			0.5	0.5
Dried potatoes	0.5	0.5	1.0	1.0
Falafel	0.5	0.5		
Lentils		0.5	0.5	
Macaroni	2.5	2.5	2.5	2.5
Instant potatoes		0.5	0.5	1.0
Refried beans	0.5	0.5	0.5	0.5
Rice	0.5	0.5	1.0	
Tortillas	1.0	1.0	1.0	1.0
Subtotal	**6.0**	**7.0**	**8.0**	**7.0**
FLOUR **% OF TOTAL LBS.**	**10%**	**10%**	**10%**	**4%**
Basic batter mix	1.5	1.5	1.5	1.0
Cornmeal	0.5	0.5	0.5	
Muffin mix	0.5		0.5	
Sweet bread mix		0.5	0.5	
Wheat	0.5	0.5	1.0	
White	0.5	0.5		1.0
Subtotal	**3.5**	**3.5**	**4.0**	**2.0**
HIGH-CALORIE, HIGH-FAT ITEMS **% OF TOTAL LBS.**	**13%**	**13%**	**13%**	**18%**
Cheese	2.0	2.0	2.0	3.5
Margarine	1.0	1.0	1.5	2.0
Meats				2.0
Oil	0.5	0.5	0.5	
Peanut butter	0.5	1.0	1.0	
Tahini				0.5
Subtotal	**4.0**	**4.5**	**5.0**	**8.0**

MUNCHABLES

% OF TOTAL LBS.	20%	20%	20%	22%
Candy	0.5	0.5	1.0	1.0
Crackers				0.5
Dried fruit	1.5	1.5	1.5	1.0
Fruit bars	1.0	0.5	1.0	1.0
High-energy bars	0.5	2.0	1.0	2.0
Pita bread				1.0
Nuts and/or seeds	1.5	1.5	1.5	1.5
Trail mix	1.0	1.0	2.0	2.0
Subtotal	**6.0**	**7.0**	**8.0**	**10.0**

DRINKS AND SUGARS

% OF TOTAL LBS.	10%	10%	10%	12%
Brown sugar	0.75	1.0	1.0	1.0
Coffee*				
Fruit crystals	0.5	0.75	1.0	1.5
Honey				
Hot chocolate	1.25	1.25	1.5	1.25
Jell-O (no NutraSweet*)		0.5	0.5	1.25
Tea bags*†	20	20	20	20
White sugar				0.5
Subtotal	**2.5**	**3.5**	**4.0**	**5.5**

DESSERTS

% OF TOTAL LBS.	3%	3%	3%	3%
Brownies		0.5		0.5
Cheesecake			0.5	0.5
Cake mix	0.5	0.5	0.5	
Pudding	0.5	0.25	0.5	0.5
Subtotal	**1.0**	**1.25**	**1.5**	**1.5**

MISCELLANEOUS

% OF TOTAL LBS.	8%	8%	8%	10%
Bouillon*	yes	yes	yes	yes
Buttermilk		0.5	0.5	
Cup-a-Soups	0.5	0.5	0.5	1.0
Dried vegetables*	yes	yes	yes	yes
Egg powder	0.5	0.5	0.5	
Instant soup mix				0.5
Milk	1.25	1.25	1.25	1.75
Miso				
Sauce mix*	yes	yes	yes	yes
Ramen soup		0.5		0.75
Tomato base	0.25	0.25	0.25	0.25
Subtotal	**2.5**	**3.0**	**3.5**	**4.25**

* You want to bring some items but not count them in your total weight, as they add no (or very few) calories.
† Number of teabags

Repackaging and Resupplying

REPACKAGING

You are not usually going to pack your food for the backcountry in the material in which it is wrapped when you purchase it. You will be repackaging, and this chapter covers that, along with setting up resupplies when your journey requires more food than you can—or want to—carry.

Repackaging Option 1: Bulk Bagging

Under Total Ration Planning, you can package food in 1- to 2-pound plastic bags without labeling the bags. It is helpful to have a small scale, but, if you don't, there is a pounds-to-cups chart in the appendix with the most commonly packed foods listed.

If you want to label the bags, go ahead—but it's really only necessary for the "white" dry goods because, even with experience, powdered milk, cheesecake, flour, couscous, grits, baking mix, and potato flakes can start to look alike, especially in the dim light of your headlamp.

Two-mil plastic bags can be tied easily in an overhand knot in the top of the bag. This works great, but remember to keep the knot loose (it will still work), and be prepared to develop a strong dislike for the first person who carries the bag by the knot, cinching it down to insufferable tightness. Some people prefer to use Ziploc bags, although they can sometimes pop open in your pack if you're not careful to remove the air from the bag and keep the food out of the zipper mechanism. It's a good idea to double-bag items such as cheese or margarine (even if they're in screw-top containers) because they can leak oil into your pack. Even bouillon cubes will melt in the heat. If you like, you can buy a bag-sealing appliance; they work great, but once you reopen the bag it becomes useless.

If the group size gets much above four or five people, plan on cooking in two groups. Otherwise the pressure on the stove is too great, and meals start taking longer and longer—which, of course, makes your companions grumpier and grumpier. Three to four people per stove is ideal.

Repackaging Option 2: Bag-a-Feast

This is more time-consuming than bulk bagging, but it will save you a lot of effort in the backcountry. Consult your daily menu and bag all ingredients needed for each individual meal into a single large plastic bag. If all ingredients are not cooked together, small bags may be needed to keep the ingredients separate until you use them. You will want to at least bag breakfasts and dinners, marking them B and D respectively (some people even number them for the specific day), and then have additional bags marked for beverages, desserts, spices, and oil/margarine. Munchables are best distributed throughout the group, with everyone packing their own.

RESUPPLYING

Time Frame

For most backcountry trips, after approximately ten days you will have to rendezvous with your resupply, or go home.

Packaging

Whatever method of resupply you choose, make sure the food is packed in weather- and animal-proof containers. Package your food so the loss of one container doesn't mean the loss of all of one type of food.

Caches

Before the trip begins, you can hide a predetermined amount of food along your route and pick it up later. It's always better if you secure your own cache, since somebody else's X on the map easily turns into a cold, hungry treasure hunt with an unhappy end result. Details are very important to note and remember. It can be difficult to find even the caches you yourself have placed. Completely clean up the cache when you're done. Leaving trash and food in the backcountry is un-cool. And since caches are illegal in many national parks and designated wilderness areas, you need to call ahead before you cache.

Sample Bag-a-Feast:
Quick Curried Rice

AT HOME: Put rice, bouillon cube, red and green peppers into a half-gallon-size plastic bag. Put chopped dried fruit, spices, and peppers into a smaller bag and seal. Put nuts and coconut in a smaller bag and seal. Put smaller bags in larger bag and seal.

IN CAMP: Pull out the bag and follow the directions in this book for Quick Curried Rice (see Entrees, page 97).

Additional Hints

- Most folks can comfortably carry an eight- to ten-day ration of food. If you pack for more than ten days, the weight starts cutting into the fun, not to mention your hips and shoulders.

- Some folks like to separate their meals into color-coded or marked bags: breakfast bag, lunch bag, and dinner bag. This works if a group always travels together, but if you don't, or you get separated from your party, you may have to eat dry elbow macaroni for lunch. If it's a paddling trip, you are well advised to divide the food types between boats. If one boat goes over and you lose a food bag, you won't lose all the candy bars or all the dinner food.

- Make sure you pack your stove and fuel well away from and below the food. A fuel leak is a terrible thing to have on top of your Lentil Chili.

- Pack several matchbooks (and a lighter) in different places in plastic bags. If you don't, and you lose your matches or they get damp, you'd better hope somebody on your trip is genetically sound enough to have packed some extra matches.

- When repackaging cheese, try not to touch it (wear gloves or plastic bags on your hands). Also, although recycling is a great thing, use fresh bags for cheese. These two things will delay mold growth.

Roadheads

You can plan your trip in a couple of big circles and resupply at your car, or have a friend meet you at a roadhead with your resupply.

Post Offices

You can mail yourself the resupply, sending it to a post office along your route. Mail it well in advance with a holding date on the label. Also, many small post offices have limited hours, so be prepared to wait . . . or call first and ask.

Commercial Packers

You can arrange for a commercial packer to deliver your resupply to you at a given place and time. Prices and weight limits vary. If you're using a commercial resupplier, make sure you get everything in writing, including the meeting point and time, and what will happen if you're late. Having the resupply dropped indiscriminately means you may spend quite a bit of time hunting for it later, a fact I must sadly report from experience. The local chamber of commerce closest to the area in which you are traveling can often send you information. Sometimes the National Park Service, US Forest Service, or Bureau of Land Management can be helpful.

Boats and Airplanes

You may be able to arrange resupply by boat if you are traveling past a major watercourse. I have been resupplied by air several times, but it's not cheap, and it is illegal in many places, such as most national parks and designated wilderness areas. The pilots generally prefer to land and hand you your resupply. This should be your first choice, too. Looking for dropped boxes that have landed in the trees is no fun, and sometimes they explode on impact.

Just Add Water:
Freeze-Dried and
Dehydrated Foods

Freeze-dried food has undergone a unique process that goes something like this: The food, cooked or fresh, gets frozen very solid, then placed in freezing temperatures with warm air flowing around it long enough for the moisture to sublimate off. Since ice crystals never form, the cells of the food remain relatively undamaged, and most of the nutrition is left intact. More than 99 percent of the food's water is removed, so the resulting product is very light in weight, with its bulk slightly reduced. Since the cells are undamaged, they rehydrate quickly and easily.

Dehydrated food is exposed to low heat in order to drive the water out. Old dehydration methods drove out a lot of nutrition as well. Newer methods preserve much of the nutritional value. A dehydrated product has 90 to 97 percent of its water removed. Dehydration shrinks the size of the cells, reducing the weight and bulk by quite a bit, and increasing the time it takes to rehydrate the food.

The quality of the rehydrated food, whether freeze-dried or dehydrated, depends primarily on its quality before the water was removed. The price of both tends to be high compared to cooking from scratch. Both products offer benefits to the backcountry chef. You can add vegetables and fruits that almost seem fresh to your dishes. You can have a quick, hot meal if you get into camp late. You can combine them with other foods to vary your diet. You can carry a few extra meals in case of an emergency without adding much weight.

FACTS AND FEELINGS
ON SOME DRIED FOODS

Serving sizes (portions) for freeze-dried/dehydrated meals vary considerably, from 3 ounces (very small) to 14 ounces (large). Most people require somewhere around 12 ounces to feel content. Be aware of serving sizes when you buy.

Adventure Food offers lots of different meals in serving sizes for two or four people, and a selection of individual food and specialty items. You can select from breakfasts, lunches, dinners, and desserts. Some meals are completely vegetarian, vegan, or gluten-free. Their website—adventurefood.com—will help you plan an expedition.

AlpineAire Foods provides a very wide variety of no-cooking-required meals, side dishes, soups, and breakfasts. It is mostly freeze-dried, but they offer some dehydrated food. Serving sizes are mostly for two people, although some meals are prepared for four, and some, for one. You can order individual items, such as meats, rice, pasta, vegetables, cheese powder, and tomato powder. They have meals for up to a year already packaged together and ready to order at alpineaire.com.

Backpacker's Pantry offers many choices of excellent meals packaged for one, two, or four people. Their full line of outdoor grub includes beverages and snacks, breakfasts, vegetarian and meat entrees, side dishes, and desserts. They also offer organic products and just-add-cold-water lunch options. On a personal note, I have consistently enjoyed the taste of meals from Backpacker's Pantry (backpackerspantry.com).

Harmony House Foods, a family-owned and operated business, is not a source of freeze-dried meals, but they do offer high-quality, freeze-dried fruits and vegetables and dehydrated vegetables, beans, and soups, along with a meat substitute flavored as ham, beef, or chicken. If you wish, you can buy in bulk and pack your own trip-size bags when you order from harmonyhousefoods.com.

Harvest Foodworks makes freeze-dried and dehydrated entrees (mostly vegetarian), desserts, breakfasts, snacks, soups, salads, and vegetables for the outdoor enthusiast. Meals come in reusable, reclosable plastic bags that contain enough grub for two. The combination of freeze-dried and dehydrated foods sometimes takes a little bit longer to prepare. The meals I tried were large and filling, and they can be ordered at harvestfoodworks.com.

Mary Janes Farm produces, among a lot of other things, a line of certified organically grown backcountry foods. Breakfasts, dinners, side dishes, breads, and desserts—all vegetarian—are available. Preparation time is longer than other outdoor specialty foods, and they're a little heavier to pack, but, uniquely, all the packaging material is completely burnable. Check out the farm at shop.maryjanesfarm.org.

Mountain House has been a truly all-freeze-dried company for more than three decades. They offer many choices in breakfasts, lunches, and dinners (including vegetarian options), desserts, snacks, and vegetables. If you want to save money, you can buy bulk items, such as twelve servings of Blueberry Cheesecake in one container. I have consistently found Mountain House tasty, although the portions are small to medium (mountainhouse.com).

Richmoor/Natural High, two brands from one company, give you a choice of traditional freeze-dried and dehydrated foods (Richmoor) or organic foods without preservatives or other additives (Natural High). There is a large selection of dinners (some vegetarian), lunches, breakfasts, desserts, vegetables, and snacks that serve two or four. Complete meals that serve four are also available. Most of the meals can be prepped in—and, for that matter, eaten from—the pouch they come in from tyry.com.

High-Energy Drinks and Bars

If you think a sudden energy boost from a drink and/or a bar sounds like a fine idea when you need the power surge for the trail, river, slope, or rope, you are correct. Here are some considerations along those lines.

HIGH-ENERGY DRINKS

It used to be that experts thought water was absorbed by your body faster than high-energy drinks. Now they say a high-energy drink, one that's up to about 6 percent carbohydrate, is actually absorbed faster than water once it reaches the small intestine. Although plain water and a high-energy drink will have the same influence on body temperature control, metabolic waste removal, and cardiovascular function in general, high-energy drinks also provide an energy boost for hardworking muscles. As an added benefit, the drinks give water a sweet (or at least interesting) taste that usually encourages consumption. During periods of moderate exercise, you can water down a high-energy drink with three or four times the recommended amount of water.

High-energy drinks also contain electrolytes, particularly sodium, potassium, and chloride, which are necessary to motivate muscles and balance fluids in your body. When you're working hard, some electrolytes, specifically sodium, are lost in your sweat. For most people, a balanced diet replaces all the electrolytes you need. But when the ambient temperature and your exercise level are high, especially when you're not acclimatized to the high heat, you'll benefit from the electrolytes in high-energy drinks.

Salt tablets should be considered a curse, and avoided. They are too strong and can irritate your stomach, cause nausea, and increase your body's need for fluid.

Facts and Feelings on
Some High-Energy Drinks

Today's market offers a great many options in high-energy drinks. I have used and appreciated the following products:

Emergen-C: Energy and electrolytes, plus 1,000 milligrams of vitamin C, in handy packets that carry one serving—and it comes in more than twenty varieties. Effervescent powder fizzes in your water bottle. If water is low, you can dump the contents straight into your mouth, but be prepared to pucker. I have downed a lot of this one (emergenc.com).

Gatorade: The original high-energy drink, this company offers—in powdered form, of course—lots of flavors that I like. You get carbohydrates and electrolytes, and it's available as G2 with half the calories for lighter exercise days. You can get it in durable packets that pack well and mix easily and in bulk containers (gatorade.com).

Phix: With all-natural ingredients, this product also offers energy drinkers sips that are vegan and free of gluten. In the mix are vitamins, minerals, green tea, and yerba mate; it comes in powder form in three flavors (that taste pretty good), packaged in single-serving sticks (phix .com).

Spark: Nutrients, vitamins, and minerals come in seven flavors, in easy-to-pack pouches or bulk canisters (if you prefer to measure out your own). Although I can't say for sure, the product also claims to boost mental focus (advocare.com).

Sqwincher: A nice balance of an energy boost and a fine flavor (ten of them, in fact) in an instant dry mix that packs well and mixes easily. The product claims to be absorbed quickly by the body, and it seems that way to me (sqwincher.com).

HIGH-ENERGY BARS

Once upon a time, there was only PowerBar. Now market shelves bend under the load of dozens of rivals in the energy bar industry. If you're facing a long day or just want a power-up snack, energy bars can provide a healthy boost. Whatever brand you choose, choose carefully. Energy bars should be no more than 25 percent, or near that, fat. Make sure the bulk of the carbohydrates are complex (rice, oats, glucose polymers, and maltodextrin, for example) for staying power, and not simple sugars.

If you're anticipating a long haul, eat a bar before you get going in order to stoke the fire of your engine. If you're pooped at the end of the long haul, eat one to restore your energy. If you need a boost, say every hour or so, take a bite of the bar. And remember that energy bars need lots of water to work their best, so drink regularly and often.

Facts and Feelings on Some High-Energy Bars

So many energy bars, so little time—and no one seems to feel exactly the same about the same bar. You'll probably want to try several. When you find your favorite, you'll probably want to stick with it. The following have been in my pack:

Balance: All bars are balanced with what they call the 40/30/30 formula—40 percent carbohydrate, 30 percent protein, 30 percent fat—a complete nutritional food. Balance Bar Gold, one option, has three layers of food, and Balance Bar Bare is advertised as more of a trail food than the others, but they all work. Taste is not bad. There are quite a few flavors (balance.com).

Clif Bar: A beefy dessert-like texture looks tasty and, by golly, it is! With a bottle of water, one of these seems like a meal. The company has a plethora of products, including an energy gel in a one-shot packet. You'll just have to visit the website to see what I mean (clifbar.com).

PowerBar: The bar that made energy bars famous now offers an array of products targeted at different needs. Harvest bars, for instance, are formulated for light to moderate levels of exercise, and Performance bars are meant for high-intensity exercise. Other examples include protein bars, recovery bars, and nutty bars. They also have an energy gel, and the taste is fine in all of the products (powerbar.com).

Promax: These hefty bars pack 20 grams of protein in with the usual mix of carbs and fats, vitamins and minerals, producing a hunk of food with a smooth texture and an okay taste. There are choices in flavors, and they also offer a Mini if you don't feel the need for a whole bar (promaxnutrition.com).

The
Backcountry
Kitchen

Setting Up
the Outdoor Kitchen

Within sixty easy paces, from one end of the clearing to the other, stand four old fire rings of blackened rocks surrounding mounds of ash, nearby earth compacted into the consistency of concrete. Not an uncommon sight, they serve as ugly reminders that camp kitchens may remain to scar the backcountry long after you're history.

An outdoor kitchen today should have as little impact on the environment as possible. Your environmentally safe kitchen ideally sits in a comfortable spot, protected from unappealing weather conditions and offering an inspiring view. It should also be an isolated spot where you won't provide an uninspiring view to other backcountry users. And it should be durable, a place that has the best chance to make the least impact on the environment.

In general, the greatest impact a kitchen makes on the backcountry comes from the destruction of vegetation and compaction of the soil, commonly resulting in erosion. Intensity of use determines much of a kitchen's impact—how many people have sat, stood, and walked around there before—but your behavior and your choice of sites will also affect your ability to leave no trace.

Concerning intensity, a heavily used spot—which means a campsite utilized more than ten times, according to the US Forest Service—does not significantly deteriorate with further use. Most of the impact comes in the first one or two times a site is used improperly. That means if you have a choice between an obviously impacted spot and a nearby pristine spot, you'll do far less damage settling where the damage has already been done. But leave it as pretty as possible. In high-use areas, you want to encourage other people to use the same site instead of creating a new one.

If you're using an unspoiled spot, choosing the cooking site ranks as the single most important consideration in terms of an environmental kitchen. First, start looking for the best site early on, before fatigue or darkness urges you to drop down in the most convenient space. If the site shows evidence of a little previous use, don't cook there. The ideal spots are without vegetation, or even soil: sand, rocks, gravel, snow. Second best are soil-based sites without vegetation. Even though your stay will cause some compaction, recovery is rapid.

If you have to choose between dense vegetation and sparse vegetation, go for the dense. Sparse plant life disturbs easier than a thick carpet of vegetation. Wet grass and dewy flowers die easily when trampled. Low shrubs and baby trees take a long time to come back from abuse. Marshy ground recovers slowly from heavy use. Dense dry grass, on the other hand (or under the other foot), makes a tough, durable surface. An open meadow of grass, even though you'll be more visible to other campers, recovers more quickly than thin vegetation hidden under a forest canopy. In short, don't rearrange the ground to suit you; find a spot that will best suit the earth, and you.

Your behavior requires more attention to details. Large parties—groups of more than four or five—have less impact if they break into smaller kitchen groups. This is especially true in more-pristine areas. Wearing soft-soled shoes around the kitchen mars the land less than boots. Reduce your movement around the kitchen as much as possible, especially in vegetated spots. Avoid making trails. Walking back and forth from tent to stove along the same path several times may leave a track that will be noticeable for years. Minimize your stay in one place; it's best for the land if you move every day.

When it's time to move on, check one more time to make sure you're packing out everything you packed in. Look for spillage at the cooking site, flour or rice that puffed out of the pot during mixing, food that fell off the plate during eating in the dark. Fluff up grass or other vegetation that got pressed down. Sprinkle duff or other natural materials over marred areas. Replace rocks or logs you may have rolled out of the way. Use a dead branch to sweep away even your tracks.

PREP AREA VERSUS COOK AREA

When you plan a lot of mixing and stirring, establish a food-preparation area apart from the cooking area. This will prevent the problem of having to start a pot of water toward boiling a second time because you knocked the first pot over.

SAFE FOOD STORAGE

Improper storage of camp food can attract unwelcome visitors—both the small ones that might eat your food, and the big ones that might eat you. Since your cooking area will be well away from your sleeping area, keeping all food in the cooking area concentrates odors in one relatively safe spot. I carry food double-bagged in plastic in a zippered duffel bag to reduce odor even more. Odorous garbage stays in the food-storage bag, in its own separate larger bag.

If the chance of a bear encounter is minimal, you can leave the food on the ground or, preferably, hang it casually from the limb of a tree. If bears frequent the area, better hang the food high. The most bear-proof hanging method requires the food bag to be suspended between two trees, a minimum of 12 feet off the ground and a minimum of 12 feet from each tree. This is a laborious process, but it's simply a great idea where bear populations are dense. You can usually get by if you haul the food bag up about 12 feet off the ground from a limb. Another option—an unbreakable bear-proof plastic container—guarantees that your food will be safe. It might be worth the money and weight if bears are thick and trees are not. In some federally managed areas, you may be required, or at least encouraged, to store your food and other attractively scented items inside a lightweight, portable, electric fence that bears seldom cross.

QUICK SUMMARY

1. Minimize environmental damage.

2. Minimize visual contact with other folks.

3. Maximize protection from unwelcome weather.

4. Maximize protection from unwelcome pests.

5. Maximize view.

Cooking the One-Burner Way

Stoves and Fuel

STOVES

Beneath every delicious one-burner meal you'll find, at some point, a one-burner stove. Your choice of stoves will help determine the outcome of meal preparation . . . and your level of frustration during cooking. Although you may not find one ideal stove for all occasions, these general tips should help you make your choice.

Weight and size: Some excellent stoves weigh far too much and take up too much room to be practical in the wilderness. Happy cooks choose a stove that packs easily and weighs little. Those committed to going as light as possible can purchase stoves weighing in at only a few ounces. Super-light stoves require a canister, but small canisters add only a few ounces more. Keep reading for quite a bit more info on one-burner stoves.

Heat output intensity and range: The more intense the heat, measured in British thermal units (BTUs), the less time it takes to boil water. Efficient stoves will boil a liter of water in three minutes (maybe less). But intense heat is not something you'll want all the time. Chefs need to be able to turn the heat down in order to simmer some fine meals.

Ease of operation: A stove that starts easily and handles easily, even in cold weather, is the stove you want.

Stability: Stoves that wobble when you set a pot on the burner are likely to dump your well-earned gourmet meal in the dirt. Choose a stove with a stable base, one that has an adequate pot-supporting surface and a relatively low profile.

Windscreens: Wind reduces the efficiency of your stove, and can snuff out the flame when you need it most. You can't control the wind, but you can choose a stove with a windscreen, or one for which you can make a windscreen.

Durability: Packs with stoves stuffed inside get dropped, sat on, stuffed into trunks of cars, and banged against trees. Choose a stove that can withstand the punishment.

Accessories: Some stoves come with a fuel bottle. That's nice. Some stoves come with a stuff sack. That's nice, too; protective sacks add to the life expectancy of your stove. Some stoves come with repair kits, another nice option. You don't want to be far from home without a stove repair kit.

Fuel used: In the United States any fuel you want is available. In many foreign countries fuel types are limited. Make sure your stove will utilize the fuel you'll have available.

Cost: The amount you pay does not necessarily indicate the efficiency of the stove for your purposes. Choose the stove that will work best for you, and then decide how to pay for it.

STOVE SAFETY AND MAINTENANCE TIPS

1. Keep your stove covered when you're not using it. Carry it in a stuff sack or kit. Keeping dirt and dust out of your stove prolongs its life and reduces maintenance.

2. Be sure your gas stove is cool before refilling. Refill outside your tent and well away from other heat sources. Use a funnel or a fuel bottle cap with a built-in pour spout to avoid spillage when refueling.

3. Fill stoves and fuel bottles that attach to stoves no more than two-thirds to three-fourths full in order to maintain air space for pressure.

4. If fuel spills on the stove during filling, allow it to evaporate before lighting.

5. Using a cover on pots while cooking reduces the amount of fuel you'll use.

6. Carry and store stoves and fuel well separated from foods.

7. Carry fuel in containers made for carrying fuel.

8. Do not burn automotive gasoline in a tent or snow cave or any enclosed area. If you must cook inside a tent or snow cave with fuel other than auto gas, light the stove outside the enclosed area, then move it inside. It is critical to make sure adequate ventilation is maintained at all times so you don't end up dead.

9. Try new stoves in your backyard before heading out on the long trail.

10. Practice taking your stove apart at home in case you have to repair it in the field.

11. Carry a stove repair kit.

FACTS AND FEELINGS ON SOME STOVES

Please note that some of the following manufacturers offer numerous models of stoves, and this list reflects only those I have used.

BioLite (biolitestove.com)

BioLite CampStove: This stove is unusual in three ways: 1) It burns twigs, pinecones, dry grass, and other combustible organic matter to generate heat for cooking (and to reduce the size of your carbon footprint); 2) it uses a unique piece of thermoelectric technology to convert heat into electric power to run a little fan that makes the stove extra efficient; and 3) it allows the unused electricity to charge small electronic gadgets such as mobile phones and LED lights. It weighs 33 ounces. The time it takes to boil a liter of water will vary depending on the available fuel, but you can probably reach the boiling point in about five minutes.

Campingaz (campingaz.com)

Bleuet 206: A compact unit, the stove weighs just shy of 10 ounces without the canister it requires. The canister will last about two hours, and it takes longer than many stoves to boil a liter of water—about five minutes. It's a bit tippy, but it's very easy to use and durable, mine lasting for many years of use.

Bleuet 206 Plus: This stove is the 206 with the addition of a stabilizer that attaches to the bottom of the canister (and works well), and a built-in windscreen (that works if the wind isn't too high). The whole thing, sans canister, weighs 13.1 ounces.

Coleman (coleman.com)

Sportster II Dual Fuel: This is a one-piece stove whose tank holds 1.1 pints of fuel. It weighs about 23 ounces empty, and is easy to use. Fairly stable, it has high heat output, and simmers great. It uses white gas or unleaded gasoline to boil a liter of water in about four minutes.

Jetboil (jetboil.com)

Sol Ti: This cooking system includes a titanium cooking cup that attaches to the stove, which attaches to a fuel canister. It weighs only 8.5 ounces if you don't count the fuel stabilizer, pot support, and measuring cup that come with it. You can boil a half-liter of water in a little over two minutes. What you gain in speed, however, you lose in options, because you can only boil water with this one.

MSR (cascadedesigns.com)

PocketRocket: This little gadget weighs only 3 ounces, screws onto a canister, includes a windscreen, and puts out enough heat to boil a liter of water in about three and a half minutes. It's easy to use, and it does allow you to simmer. The pot you balance on the relatively small top requires attention to prevent an accident.

WhisperLite: This stove attaches to a bottle of liquid fuel (white gas) and comes with a fuel pump, windscreen, heat reflector, repair kit, and stuff sack. It weighs 14.5 ounces. It's easy to use as liquid-fuel stoves go, works well in cold weather, and it's quiet (as the name implies). It produces high heat that boils a liter of water in about four minutes, but adjusts to simmer a meal as well. The unit is stable and folds up to pack neatly inside many pots. I've beat mine up a lot, but it keeps on working.

WhisperLite International: Very much like the WhisperLite, this multi-fuel stove burns white gas, kerosene, and automotive gasoline (unleaded).

DragonFly: This liquid-fuel unit burns white gas, kerosene, unleaded automotive gas, diesel, and even jet fuel. Wide pot supports provide excellent stability, but it will fold up and pack in a 2-liter pot. It weighs 14 ounces, and, burning white gas, it will boil a liter of water in three and a half minutes. You can easily and fully adjust flame, from low simmer to rapid boil, making this an excellent choice for the backcountry gourmet. It's a favorite of mine.

XGK-EX: Tough and powerful, even when the temperature plunges and the altitude soars, the XGK delivers high heat, bringing a liter of water to boil in under three minutes with kerosene in the bottle. It's stable, fairly easy to use, and burns almost all types of fuel. The weight runs around 13.2 ounces. You can't simmer with this one, but it's my favorite mountaineering stove.

Optimus (optimusstoves.com)

Hiker: This stove is stable, must be primed, and works well in wind and cold. The unit folds up into a heavy but very durable 7-by-7-inch box, and weighs in at about 54 ounces. It has adjustable intensity, with great simmering ability, and burns white gas, kerosene, or alcohol. A proven performer in the arena of one-burners.

Svea: Compact and durable, a bit tippy, this stove works well at higher altitudes but performs less well in cold. It must be primed, and burns only white gas. It loses efficiency without a windscreen, and weighs in at 19.5 ounces, including a lid that serves as a small pot. It takes about seven minutes to boil a liter of water (but remember, this one has been available for more than a hundred years!).

Primus (primuscamping.com)

OmniLite Ti: A liquid-fuel stove, this one is small, fuel-efficient, and light (largely due to a lot of titanium parts), weighing 12 ounces. Adjustable, you can simmer or blast with the flame—boiling a liter of water in about two and a half minutes—and you can burn almost any fuel. It attaches to a fuel bottle and comes with a fuel pump, windscreen, heat reflector, fuel bottle, repair tool, and storage sack. This unit might be too small for four to five people, but it works great for a couple of back-country eaters.

ExpressStove Ti Kit: A little 3.3-ounce stove that screws onto a canister, it will boil a liter of water in three and a quarter minutes, and it comes in a little bag with a pot that holds about a liter. It's fairly stable, and a good choice for one or two people.

YOUR STOVE IN THE COLD OUTDOORS

When it gets really cold, neither you nor your stove is going to function optimally. Some stoves will require preheating. Some stoves won't work at all, especially some of the canister types. If you plan to cook outside in winter conditions, make sure you know your stove's capabilities.

YOUR STOVE AT HIGH ALTITUDE

When you go up in altitude, the amount of oxygen you and your stove take in with each breath goes down. At 18,000 feet the oxygen in the ambient air is only about half what it is at sea level. That means the efficiency of your stove goes down. If there's not enough oxygen for your stove to burn all the fuel being released, the flame will be cooler and yellower. If you plan to go high, make sure, once again, that you know your stove's capabilities.

And remember, water boils at a lower temperature the higher you go, which adds to the inefficiency. It takes longer to cook food at altitude, which means you'll need more fuel, so plan accordingly.

FUELS

Here is a list of different fuel options for stoves:

- **Alcohol:** Heat output is low, and flammability is high. This fuel burns clean, and spills evaporate quickly without leaving a harmful residue.
- **Automotive gasoline:** Use unleaded only; leaded gas produces toxic fumes when burned. Explosions are possible. Heat output and flammability are high. Stoves may clog with prolonged use.
- **Butane:** This fuel burns clean, and is easy and safe to use. It must be carried in canisters, most of which can't be changed until they're empty, and heat output goes down as fuel runs low. Heat output is reduced by cold temperatures (must be kept above freezing).
- **Propane:** This fuel burns clean, and is easy and safe to use. It must be carried in canisters, and performs fairly well in cold weather (if it doesn't freeze).
- **Butane/propane mix:** This fuel burns clean, and is easy and safe to use. It must be carried in canisters, and performs fairly well at high altitudes and in cold temperatures.
- **Kerosene:** The heat output is high, but flammability is the lowest of all fuels; however, it has a strong smell. If you spill it, some of it remains oily, unlike other fuels, which evaporate quickly.

- **White gas (or naphtha):** This fuel burns clean, and is much cheaper than canisters of fuel. Heat output is high, as is flammability; explosions are possible. Works well at high altitudes and in cold weather, although preheating the burner might be required.

Tips for Figuring Liquid Fuel Needs
- On summer trips, figure one-sixth of a liter per person per day; that's three-sixths (or a half-liter) per person for a three-day trip, and 1 liter per person for a six-day trip.
- On fall and spring trips, figure a fourth of a liter per person per day, especially if you're traveling in a cold climate and/or at higher altitudes.
- On winter trips and at high altitude, figure a half-liter per person per day, especially if you're melting snow for water (better safe than sorry).

Gear for
the Outdoor Kitchen

As every cook and carpenter knows, one of the big secrets of a great product is using the right tool for the job. In the backcountry, gourmet meals can be prepared with a minimum of simple cooking gear, but it should be thoughtfully chosen for maximum chef appeal.

POTS AND PANS

Material

Lightweight and least expensive, cookware made from **aluminum** is the most likely to be pulled from an outdoor kitchen bag. You may have heard stories about how aluminum flakes off into food, but not enough would ever flake off your outdoor pots to cause a health problem. If the aluminum has been anodized, it got an acid bath and a jolt of electricity to make the metal a lot stronger. For those bored with the dull gray of standard pots and pans, some manufacturers offer anodized aluminum coated with a heat-sealed color, such as a pleasant maroon with Evolution cookware from Backpacker's Pantry (backpackerspantry .com), or black with BlackLite from MSR (cascadedesigns.com/msr). It's a nice touch, but the real plus is the nonstick coating on the inside and the lighter-than-ever weight.

Stainless-steel pots cost more and weigh a little more, but they hold up better, generally speaking, under outdoor abuse, and they're a bit easier to clean. They conduct heat a little more slowly than aluminum. Some outdoor stainless-steel pots have copper on the bottom to increase heat conductivity. Primus (primuscamping.com) and MSR (cascadedesigns. com/msr) offer some great stainless-steel products

Then there is **titanium,** a high-tech metal with a greater strength-to-weight ratio than any other outdoor cookware. If you're the kind of cook who'll cut the handles off spoons to save weight, 1) you're silly, and 2) you'll love titanium. Beware: It does not heat as evenly as stainless steel or aluminum, the thin walls dent easier, and it definitely costs the most. Once again, check out MSR's cookware.

A great advance in one-burner cooking comes from Primus, and it's called Eta cookware. The pots involve both hard **anodized aluminum and titanium** (so expect to pay a premium price), but a heat exchanger attached to the bottom of the pots cuts down cooking time by about a third. They come in five sizes (primuscamping.com).

Enamel cookware, although functional and colorful, chips and rusts too easily for me. It is quite safe to use outdoors, the metals under enamel being inert (which means they won't affect your health if you swallow some).

Nonstick coatings, such as Teflon, on pots and pans are also made from inert materials. If you choose a nonstick coating for your outdoor cookware, don't worry about chips and don't worry about the coating when it rubs off in spots. Chips will pass harmlessly through your digestive tract, if you swallow one, and there's no health reason to discard pots and pans with worn surfaces.

Size and Type

Depending on the length of trip and number of people, you'll probably want to own a set of pots ranging in size from 1 to 4 liters. You'll decide your needs and carry those pots necessary to do the job for a particular trip. Even when there are only two of you, you may want to carry two pots: one to boil water in and one to cook in, or one to mix in and one to cook in. Buy sets that nest together for pack-ability. Some people prefer pots with handles, but sometimes the handles get so hot that I end up using pot grips anyway. It is important that all pots have a lid that fits well. Lids make cooking faster, hold in heat while you're waiting, and reduce the amount of pine needles and grit in your food. Make sure you choose pots with a very limited number of plastic parts, zero being the optimal number.

One pan approximately 10 inches in diameter, the deeper the better (say, 2 inches), with a nonstick surface, is a must for fine cooking. Choose one with a lid. Once again, some people like pans with a folding handle, but you can use pot grips for a handle-less pan, too. My personal favorite is the Banks Fry-Bake pan, an aluminum pan with an anodized hard coat for easy cleaning and great durability. It comes in two sizes: the 10.5-inch-diameter Expedition, perfect for a meal for two, and the 8-inch-diameter Alpine, intended for one, but you can crowd in enough for two (frybake.com). Their snug-fitting lids allow you to build a twiggy fire on top if baking requires one.

Pressure cookers can cut cooking time for things like beans almost in half. For high-altitude trips, you'll save lots of time and fuel. Backcountry versions are available, including a couple of models from GSI Outdoors, that work very well. GSI's smallest pressure cooker, however—2.7 liters and 2.0 pounds 12 ounces—adds bulk and a chunk of weight to a backpack (gsioutdoors.com).

Coffee percolators just right for one-burner stoves and mini espresso makers are available from several manufacturers, such as GSI Outdoors. As a lover of a fine cup of coffee, I've been happy with my Big Sky Bistro, a French press integrated into a 16-ounce insulated mug (planetarydesign.us). But I'm not opposed to good old "cowboy coffee," and it can still be made in any old pot.

Outback Oven

For easy, high-quality baking on a one-burner stove, nothing beats the Outback Oven from Backpacker's Pantry (backpackerspantry.com). It's not totally foolproof, but with a little practice, you'll be able to turn out fabulous breads, pizza, and desserts. I've used the Outback Oven, regular version, with a 10-inch diameter, and the Ultralight, with an 8-inch diameter. You'll get a diffuser plate and riser bars to create hot air out of your stove's energy, a fabric convection dome to trap the hot air around your personal pan or pot, and a thermometer to monitor baking temperatures. The accessories are also sold separately. Backpacker's Pantry offers a line of food mixes prepared especially for the Outback Oven.

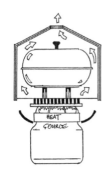

BakePacker

For the ultimate in simple baking, try the BakePacker (bakepacker.com). You just put mixed ingredients in a plastic (yes, plastic) bag, place the bag in your pot on top of the BakePacker, make sure enough water has been added to the pot to cover the cells of the oven, and boil. Because the food is

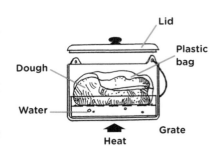

steam-baked, you don't get crusty tops, but the system works, and messy post-baking cleanup is eliminated.

KITCHEN ACCESSORIES

You'll probably be sorry if you don't have a large spoon to stir and serve with, and maybe a spatula. Pot grips are useful, but I typically carry a smallish Leatherman multi-tool with pliers that work as pot grips, a knife, can opener, and other often-handy attachments (leatherman. com). You'll need some plastic containers in various sizes for things such as butter or cooking oil, and spices. Be warned that the Environmental Protection Agency (EPA) advises against using 35mm plastic film canisters for foodstuffs, since the plasticizers may rub off into your food. Leftover plastic containers that once contained butter or the like do work, but they sometimes pop open in your pack. I generally prefer containers with screw-on tops. (Hint: If you have small spice/salt/pepper containers with screw-on tops, measure how much the top holds in order to use that measurement later.) Optional items include a small wire whisk, a measuring cup, an abrasive pad for cleanup, and large collapsible water container to keep water readily available in the kitchen.

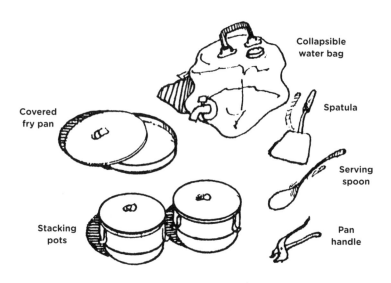

Collapsible water bag

Covered fry pan

Spatula

Serving spoon

Stacking pots

Pan handle

A lot of the frenetic bother of searching for smaller kitchen items can be eliminated by purchasing one of several options in kitchen-organizer kits. You might find inside, depending on the kit, Lexan knives, forks, and spoons, a serving spoon, whisk, can opener, spatula, scrubber, collapsible measuring cup, and containers of various sizes for spices and such. Look for pockets that will allow you to pack personal additions. One source for great choices is GSI Outdoors (gsioutdoors.com).

PERSONAL ITEMS

Everyone needs a personal mug, and I prefer the plastic insulated travel variety, 12 to 16 ounces, with snap-on lid. Drinks in metal cups seem to always be too hot or too cold. When you know the capacity, they can be used as guesstimators for measuring. To reduce the guesswork, mark your travel mug before your trip. You see these mugs for sale everywhere. Your personal water bottle can be purchased with measuring grids pre-marked by the manufacturer.

A personal bowl is needed when a group travels together. A couple of people can eat out of the pots and pans—with probably a germ or two being shared along with the cookware. An unbreakable plastic spoon is needed for eating . . . unless you want to carve some chopsticks, which I've done when somehow the spoons got left at home. (Hint: If you measure your spoon to see how much it holds, you might find that measurement useful later.)

Here's a personal outdoor kitchen gear checklist:
- Personal cup
- Personal bowl
- Personal spoon
- Leatherman (for knife, pot grips, can opener)
- 1- and 2-liter pots with lids
- Banks Fry-Bake pan with lid
- Large collapsible water container
- Kitchen organizer kit with small containers, spatula, large spoon, wire whisk, and scrubbing pad
- Backpacker's Pantry large convection dome (made for the Outback Oven)

Camp Kitchen Hygiene

Germs (bacteria, viruses, parasites) are responsible for illnesses, including yucky stomachs and the early retirement of more backcountry chefs than all other reasons combined. Many germs commonly lurk in backcountry water. Others proliferate in food that's been improperly cooked or stored. Some germs live long, successful lives on human skin, even healthy humans, without bothering those people. But when some of those same germs fall off into breakfast, lunch, or dinner preparations, they multiply with great speed and lead to disease. Unhealthy people carry germs that can often be passed easily by hand and mouth. And humans have germs living in their bowels, which they share—disgusting but true—in the camp kitchen when they fail to adequately wash their hands after a bowel movement. You do *not* want germs as guests at any meal.

WATER DISINFECTION

Many invisible bacteria, viruses, and parasites find a home in water, and all wilderness water sources should be eyed with suspicion in relation to health. It's not the big stuff in water that makes you sick, but water with a lot of visible sediment in it should be strained. You can strain it through anything that will trap sediment while letting water pass through (bandanna, T-shirt, paper coffee filter). But good camp kitchen hygiene requires safe water, and there are, basically, four ways to ensure the quality of water.

Heat: Killing all the microorganisms in water, a process known as sterilization, requires five to ten minutes of boiling at sea level. But not all microorganisms cause illness. Take heat-resistant bacterial spores; they're harmless. Pasteurization, the process of bringing a liquid to almost boiling, works toward killing everything in water that can make a human sick. *Giardia* dies in two to three minutes at 158 degrees Fahrenheit. Viruses die in seconds at 176° F. By the time water reaches the boiling point, worldwide, it's safe to drink, even at an altitude of 19,000 feet, where the boiling point of water is 178° F. Water used to cook with does not have to be disinfected prior to use, as the cooking process will disinfect it.

Chemicals: Iodine and chlorine are good chemical water disinfectants readily available in easily packed forms for the backcountry. When used properly, they'll kill most parasites, viruses, and bacteria. They have not, however, been proven effective against *Cryptosporidia*, and they are not always especially effective at killing *Giardia*. A third chemical, chlorine dioxide, completely kills all germs, but the wait time, depending on how safe you want the water to be, can be four hours long. The effectiveness of these chemicals depends on their concentration in the water and the amount of time you wait before drinking. In other words, you can reduce the amount of the chemical if you're willing to wait longer for it to work. Remember that cold water slows the effect of chemical disinfectants, so in cold water you should use more, or wait longer. When opting for chemical use, the safest approach is buying a commercial product and following the instructions. If you're carrying chemical disinfectants, use them in all of your drinking water and wait until they have acted before adding anything to the water to sweeten or flavor it, since additional sugars and such will interfere with the process of disinfection.

Filtration: Backcountry water filters come in many forms and many levels of efficacy. Some remove everything removable; some remove little more than leaves and fish. Many backcountry water filters remove protozoan life forms and bacteria, but none will remove viruses. Some filters kill viruses via contact with an iodine resin on the filter. Read the labels carefully before buying so that you know what the filter does and how to use it to ensure that it does what the product claims to do.

Ultraviolet Light: Ultraviolet light has long been recognized as a means to disinfect water, but no practical application was available until sort of recently. Now you can purchase a handheld device, light enough in weight to be easily packed, that operates on AA batteries and quickly makes a liter of water safe from viruses, bacteria, and protozoa. The UV light emitted by the device destroys the DNA of microbes, rendering them unable to reproduce. No reproduction of germs equates with no illness in humans. And there is no risk of harm to humans from the UV light. A UV light device, in general, costs more but offers the shortest route to safe water.

FACTS AND SOME FEELINGS ON A FEW WATER FILTERS

First Need XL Water Purifier: This 0.1 micron carbon matrix filter is fairly lightweight, good quality, relatively easy to use—and fast (pumps, says the manufacturer, 1.8 liters per minute). The pre-filter strains out large debris, and the filter eliminates protozoans, bacteria, and viruses without chemicals. Also removes chemical contaminants, bad tastes, and nasty odors. This filter can be cleaned in the field, and the EPA has approved it as a water purifier (generalecology.com).

Katadyn Hiker Water Filter: Pleated cartridge with 0.3 micron glass fiber removes protozoa and bacteria—but not viruses. The pre-filter keeps out larger particulate matter, and it pumps fairly easily, at about 1 liter per minute. Lightweight and very popular, this was a PUR filter before Katadyn took over (katadyn.com).

Katadyn Vario Water Filter: This is a dependable, durable, precisely manufactured Swiss product, with the look and feel of a fine tool. Ceramic, adjustable pre-filter keeps out large stuff; the glass fiber filter eliminates protozoans and bacteria without chemicals; the active charcoal gets rid of odors. The company that makes this filter says it is easy to use and can pump 2 liters per minute, without the pre-filter; however, viruses can get through (katadyn.com).

MSR MiniWorks EX Microfilter: This filter has a ceramic/carbon element with 0.2 micron pore size, which removes protozoa and bacteria. Viruses can get through. Carbon absorbs chemicals and particles that smell or taste bad. Long lever makes it easy to pump, and the filter pushes through about 1 liter per minute. It can be cleaned in the field, and its durable construction promises a long life (cascadedesigns.com/msr).

SweetWater Purifier System: Microfilter removes protozoa and bacteria, and improves taste and odor of water. You can add the chlorine-based purifier solution to deactivate viruses, resulting in very safe water. The pump handle offers 4:1 ratio for easy pumping of about 1.25 liters per minute. It can be cleaned in the field (cascadedesigns.com/msr).

HAND WASHING

All good cooks have at least one thing in common: clean hands. Your outer layer of skin is an overlapping armor of dead cells that protects the living cells beneath. Under a microscope this outer layer looks like the surface of the Colorado Plateau from 30,000 feet: canyons and mesas, cracks and fissures. Resident microbes are wedged firmly into the low spots. Some of these microbes are friendly, serving to keep skin slightly acid and resistant to other microbial life forms such as fungi. Others can make you severely sick. In addition to the residents, transient germs come and go as fortune dictates. They can accumulate rapidly after bowel movements, and they congregate most thickly under fingernails and in the deeper fissures of fingertips. That's why human hands account for 25 to 40 percent of all foodborne illness.

Hand washing prior to food handling, even with detergents, does not remove all the flora, but it does significantly reduce the chance of contamination. For your information, science recommends the following eight-step hand-washing technique for maximum cleanliness:

1. Wet hands with hot flowing water (100 to 120° F).

2. Soap up until a good lather is attained.

3. Work the lather all over the surface of the hand, concentrating on fingernails and tips.

4. Clean under fingernails.

5. Rinse thoroughly with hot water (very important).

6. Re-soap and re-lather.

7. Re-rinse.

8. Dry with a paper towel (very important) to wipe off bacteria clinging to the water.

For most of us, hot water is a rare wilderness commodity. But you can still get clean hands with this modified, seven-step, backcountry technique, which substitutes germicidal soap for hot water. In tests, adequate hand sanitation was achieved with as little as a half-liter of water. Move at least 200 feet away (70 adult paces) from the source of water when using any soap in the wilderness.

1. Wet hands thoroughly.

2. Add a small amount of germicidal soap (such as Klenzade, Betadine Scrub, or Hibiclens).

3. Work lather up, especially on fingertips.

4. Clean under fingernails (and keep your nails trimmed).

5. Rinse thoroughly.

6. Repeat soap, lather, and rinse.

7. Dry with a small clean towel or bandanna.

Hand Sanitizers

In a rush? Join the crowd, but not the sick crowd. Some products provide quick hand sanitization with a fast but thorough rub-and-let-dry. They work, but they are often made with alcohol or other rather potent chemicals that can be harsh to your skin with constant use. You can combat the harshness by using a product with moisturizers. And I recommend a good hand washing with soap and water at least once a day even if you're using the quick fix of chemicals.

FOOD HANDLING

Wilderness food usually shows up in plastic bags, and food contamination can be further reduced by pouring the food out instead of reaching in for it. It ought to go without saying, but here it is anyway: Already-sick people should stay out of the kitchen.

Some well-cooked backcountry food doesn't get the opportunity to be processed by the human digestive system. This results from cooking more than you can eat, which is a result, most often, of less-than-maximal meal-planning skills. Storage of cooked-but-uneaten food in the wilderness poses an almost insurmountable problem. Bacteria grow optimally at temperatures ranging from 45 to 90° F, and unhealthy populations of bacteria can be reached in a brief period of time. A tuna sandwich on a warm day can become dangerous in less than four hours. Reheating cooked food, although it kills bacteria, often leaves dangerous toxins, produced by the bacteria, at sickening levels. Your safest bet is not to eat leftovers unless the air is winter cold and the food loses its heat very fast—and you'll still need to thoroughly reheat it before eating.

A CLEAN KITCHEN IS A HEALTHY KITCHEN

Another major source of food contamination in the wilderness is dirty cookware and kitchen utensils. Your choice of cookware—say, aluminum versus stainless steel—and utensils—say, wood versus plastic—is irrelevant in terms of germs, but cookware should be washed and dried daily, and utensils should be cleaned prior to use in the preparation and serving of food. An exception would be extremely cold conditions in which food residue freezes before you can wash it off.

PACK IT IN, PACK IT OUT

As any sanitation engineer can tell you, much can be learned about people by going through their garbage. The same goes for backcountry trash; in the plus column, the amount of litter has steadily decreased in wilderness areas over the last twenty years, despite an increase in litter bearers. But the potential impact of trash ranks low as a health hazard, while the disposition of leftover food and, far more important, human waste products, ranks as the greatest risk.

WHAT TO DO WITH YOUR DOO

You can't realistically pack out everything you pack in, except in special circumstances (such as dragging frozen feces off winter trips), but you can, with an adequate poo-poo plan, reduce the risk of fecal contamination to an absolute minimum. Transmission of fecal borne pathogens occurs in four ways: direct contact with the feces (even using toilet paper leaves germs on your hands); indirect contact with hands that have directly contacted the feces; contact with insects that have contacted the feces; and drinking water contaminated with feces.

Human waste products break down to a harmless state as a result of two mechanisms: 1) bacterial action in the presence of oxygen, moisture, and warmth, and 2) inactivation from direct ultraviolet radiation and dryness. Deposition of solid body wastes should include placement to maximize decomposition, to minimize the chance of something or someone finding it, and to minimize the chance of water contamination. And after the deed, wash your hands.

Latrines are out, except in established spots. They concentrate too much poop in one place. They carry a high risk of water pollution. They invite insect and mammal investigation. They are unsightly, and they stink. If you are ever required to dig a latrine, make it at least a foot deep, add soil after each deposit, and fill it in when the total excreta lies several inches below the surface.

For years, environment- and health-concerned wildland managers have recommended cat holes as the best way to manage human feces. Preferably in a level spot, a cat hole should be dug several inches into an organic layer of soil, where decomposing microorganisms live most abundantly. After you've dropped your droppings, stir them into the soil to speed decomposition. Cover the mess with a couple of inches of soil, and disguise the spot to hide it from later passersby.

Although urine contains, normally, an insignificant number of bacteria, it can carry, almost always in developing countries, parasites such as schistosomes. To stay on the safe side, urinate on rocks or in non-vegetated spots far from water sources and your kitchen whenever possible . . . unless otherwise directed by a wildland manager, who may ask you to pee in a river or lake. Urine on the rocks keeps animals from creating an unsightly excavation later.

CARE—BUT DON'T ALWAYS SHARE

Nice people are willing to share, but they may be passing around more than their water bottle. Keep your lip balm and your toothbrush to yourself. Personal eating utensils and mugs should stay personal. If you can't finish your candy bar or your lunch, dispose of the leftovers properly instead of passing your germs along to someone else.

QUICK SUMMARY

1. Disinfect all water.

2. Keep your hands clean.

3. Don't save leftovers overnight—unless it's cold.

4. Wash and dry your cooking gear and personal utensils daily.

5. Pack it in, pack it out.

6. Have a hygienic poo-poo plan.

7. Don't share too much.

Recipes and Secrets of Backcountry Cooking

Cooking Tips and Other Bits of Friendly Advice

Details, and the attention paid to them, separate someone who merely boils water from someone worthy of the title "backcountry chef."

SPICE UP YOUR LIFE

The spice kit is the backcountry chef's friend—sometimes a best friend. I bring an extensive spice kit when using the Total Food Rationing plan, and a limited one even when carrying primarily prepackaged foods.

The spice kit is the easiest way to make a good friend or a worst enemy. Remember to add spices a little bit at a time. Some spices, like the peppers, increase in strength as they cook, so wait a while between dashes. (A dash is less than a pinch; a pinch is about an eighth of a teaspoon.) It's relatively easy to go from the flavor of cardboard to red-hot chili-pepper fire if you're not paying attention.

Use a spoon or a shaker lid to add your spices to food. A whole canister of accidental curry is hard to choke down (even on potatoes). And your hands are dirty utensils. Take heed: Rubbing your eye with cayenne is no fun.

If worse comes to worst, spices can be added to individual portions, which is especially useful if you have a companion who has had his "hot" buds surgically removed.

Don't carry your spices in film canisters. Yes, it's a handy size, but they're not safe for food unless you like eating plastic. Many small canisters are commercially available (some are even sold with the spices in them!), or you can use baby bottle bags and tie a loose knot in the top. Label your spices if you want.

Once they're individually packaged, carry all your spices together in a single bag—your spice kit.

Popular Spices and Their Common Uses

Baking powder: Buy double-acting; this white powder is used as a leavening agent in quick breads, cakes, and biscuits.

Baking yeast: Light brown granules used in yeast bread recipes.

Basil: Dark green, chopped leaves that smell sweet. Great in tomato and cream sauces. Use this often on pasta, pizzas, and potatoes.

Black pepper: Looks sort of like ground-up rock. You can put this on almost every dish you make to enhance the flavor—and that's why it's the world's most popular spice. Probably aids in digestion, too.

Cayenne: Ground red pepper; this neon-red powder is very hot, so be careful.

Chili pepper: Deep red granules. Spicy; used mostly in Mexican dishes.

Cinnamon: Fine brown powder with a strong sweet smell. Great in porridge, sweet breads, cobblers, and cakes.

Crushed red pepper: Red flakes with bits of yellow. Very hot; use with caution.

Cumin powder: Greenish-brown powder used in many Mexican dishes. Especially good on beans. This spice is commonly confused with curry powder.

Curry powder: A gold powder with a strong smell and taste; different kinds have different flavors. Can be hot and spicy if you use enough, and food turns gold when you sprinkle it on. (At that point it's too late to turn back.) Used commonly in rice and fruit dishes.

Dill weed: Looks like chopped thin grass and smells like a sweet perfume. Good in creamy soups and sauces and breads.

Garlic powder: Pale yellowish white granules; smells like garlic! Adds flavor to almost all dishes and keeps vampires away; an eighth of a teaspoon equals about one clove of fresh garlic.

Mrs. Dash: Comes commercially in a variety of mixes. Great on fish or any casserole to perk it up quickly. Lemon and garlic flavors are particular hits.

Mustard: Bright yellow powder that tastes like a hot mustard. Good in cream sauces, pasta, and bean dishes.

Onion flakes: Hard white flakes that smell like onion. These need to be hydrated to be used for their best potential. One tablespoon equals about half a medium onion.

Oregano: Light green leaf bits. Smells strong and tastes slightly bitter, but it enhances many dishes. Great in Italian food. Often mistaken for basil, but they interchange so nicely it really doesn't matter.

Parsley flakes: Greenish leafy bits. Kind of a fresh grass taste, but it works in food. Good in pasta or grain dishes or sprinkled on fish.

Salt: White granules. Tastes like salt! Salt can be added into almost all recipes, but is not a required ingredient. If your food tastes bland or "soapy," it's probably because you need a little salt. Salt brings out the flavor. Remember: Instant soups, bouillon, soy, and tamari all contain salt, as do most prepackaged meals. Salt is not a "bad" thing nutritionally; in fact, you need salt to function healthily. Too much salt may sometimes be a problem for folks who have hypertension.

SOME CONDIMENTS

Hot sauces: These come in a variety of brands. Pick your favorite and bring a small plastic bottle along, especially on extended journeys.

Soy sauce or tamari: Salty, dark liquid that is great in soups and sauces, over grains and lentils. Good on popcorn. Can be purchased in a powdered form.

Vanilla extract: A brown liquid that smells sweet and is useful in baking and frostings. Nice addition to hot cereals and hot drinks.

Vinegar: Clear or wine-colored, this tangy liquid has a large number of applications. Useful in sweet-and-sour, salsa, and peanut-butter sauces.

THICKENING AGENTS

Utilizing the crude measuring methods typically available in the backcountry, sometimes your soups, sauces, and even your entrees can end up too watery. Try any of the following ingredients to thicken your food and save things that become too soupy: flour, potato flakes, an egg and milk powder mix, or even instant cereals. (It's usually best to mix them into a paste with water and then add them, a practice that prevents, or at least limits, the chance of lumps. This works for tomato powder as well. If you use thickening agents often, a small whisk will make the job easier, with better results.)

SPEEDING UP COOKING TIME

- Choose a sheltered spot for the stove and use a wind shield, especially if it's windy. Heating the outdoors with a one-burner stove is a big project, and you'll get hungry while you try. Many stoves are packaged with a wind shield, or you can purchase them separately or improvise one using aluminum foil. Using the convection dome (or "Pot Parka") from Backpacker's Pantry also traps heat (backpackerspantry.com), and some pot sets are marketed with an optional heat exchanger. These can save a lot of time and fuel, especially on cold, high-altitude trips.
- Cooking with a lid cuts down on cooking time. Don't lift the lid or stir too often, as this reduces the temperature, making for a longer cooking time.
- Presoaking dehydrated vegetables and beans throughout the day can save time. A water bottle works well for this. If you overhydrate hash browns, they turn to mush. To test for hydration, break a portion in half and look for dryness in the middle. If it's dry, it's not hydrated. Do not presoak pasta!

PREVENTING BURNAGE

- If you are a beginner, the best way to prevent burning is to make sure you don't leave the kitchen while you're cooking. A watched pot *will* boil, despite claims to the contrary—and even claims in this book.
- Make sure you use plenty of water; you can always add thickener later. Bring dishes to a boil, then reduce them to a simmer and stir occasionally. Add more water if needed; sticky is better than burnt.
- Milk and cheese like to burn, so add them last and watch them carefully.
- Margarine and oil burn less readily than butter. Margarine also spoils less readily than butter, so it's doubly good.
- When you're frying, it's okay to add a little water to help cook the ingredients and prevent burning—but it does cut down on the crispy factor.

- To prevent burning when baking, make sure your stove is on a low simmer and rotate the Fry-Bake pan frequently. To adjust the heat, hold your hand about 10 inches over the flame. You should be able to keep your hand there but still feel the heat. Keep as much heat as you want on the top of the pan while baking. Oil and flour the bottom of the Fry-Bake pan liberally. If you start to smell a strong, wonderful aroma—or burning—it's time to check.

PREVENTING ACCIDENTS

- Keep everyone but the cook out of the kitchen. If it's too crowded, people kick things over and dinner ends up in the dirt. Even worse, boiling water ends up in someone's lap, or boot.
- If you have to cook under a tarp or tent vestibule, at least fill and light your stove somewhere far away. Nylon melts really quickly, even when it's raining. And ventilate the cook area well; dying from carbon monoxide poisoning puts a damper on future trips.
- Keep water handy. Twiggy fires gone wild and stoves kicked over can burn down the forest, and you with it.
- Don't pour hot water into handheld containers. Burns are one of the leading causes of backcountry evacuations.
- Don't use your leg or any other part of your body as a cutting board. When using a knife, cut away from yourself.
- Fill your stove after it cools, and after every meal. If you have an emergency, your stove will always be ready.

TIPS FOR COLD-WEATHER COOKING

- Camp early. Cooking in the cold darkness lowers the fun factor. It also makes it harder to cook effectively.
- Shelter is even more important in the cold. If there's deep snow on the ground, stamping or digging out a kitchen area (that can be filled in when you leave) not only makes for a great, sheltered place to cook, but it also warms you up at the same time.
- Make a lot of hot drinks. They're a great source of calories, and they make people happy.

- Bring a light pair of gloves to wear while cooking. When it's "wicked" cold out, merely touching your stove can cause a nasty tissue injury. Avoid spilling fuel on flesh, which can cause rapid frostbite.
- Wipe the snow off the pots before placing them on the stove. The water dripping on the burner causes flame inconsistencies.
- Cut your cheese, meats, and margarine into chunks before leaving home. Even if they freeze solid, you can still break off some chunks . . . probably.
- Put your munchables in the inside pocket of your parka. Food might remain unfrozen at snack time.
- When melting snow for water, always keep some starter water. Snow melts faster in water. There is more surface area. Go to bed with a liter of hot chocolate in your thermos; it's pleasant to snuggle up to, and you can drink it during the night for a calorie boost.
- Sleep with snacks in winter. Those twelve-hour winter nights are a long time to go without eating.

Breakfasts

When the trail, climbing route, or river beckons, breakfast is even more deserving of the title "Most Important Meal of the Day."

"NO TIME FOR BREAKFAST" BREAKFASTS

CHEESY MASH

SERVES 1

$^2/_3$ to $^3/_4$ cup hot water
2–3 tablespoons dry milk
1 glob margarine
$^2/_3$ cup potato flakes
$^1/_4$ cup cheese in small bits
Garlic powder, chili powder, salt, and pepper to taste

Heat water, milk, and margarine. Stir in potato flakes and cheese until just moist. Let stand for 30 to 60 seconds. Add spices and eat. (Note: This works at lower elevations, too.)

QUESADILLAS A LA TAMAH

SERVES 3–4

1 dozen flour tortillas
1 pound pepper jack cheese (shredded at home)

Fiddle with your stove for ten minutes while swearing. Look for your stove-cleaning kit and then realize you left it at home. Prime your stove and then realize there is only a little fuel left in it, so you'll have to start all over again. Heat your frying pan (over that stove you love so much). Put a tortilla in the pan; put some cheese on the tortilla. Wait for the cheese to melt. Fold the tortilla in half, pull it out of the pan, and eat it immediately while telling your partner that the next one is his or hers.

Variations: Add hydrated tomatoes, green pepper, or salsa.

Thanks to Tamah V. Donaldson, Cal Adventures, Berkeley, California

BREAKFAST IN BED (FOR ONE)

SERVES 1

1 cup quick oatmeal
4 tablespoons dry milk
Small handful raisins and nuts
$\frac{1}{2}$ tablespoon brown sugar
2 cups boiling water

Make this in a thermos before bedding down. Snuggle up to the thermos in your sleeping bag, and in the morning you'll have breakfast in bed. The cereal will stay relatively warm if you make it in a water bottle that has an insulated cover. Hey, it's better than getting up!

Variations: Convince someone to bring you a cup of hot chocolate to have with your oatmeal.

Popular Variations on the Theme

Leftovers: Make too much dinner and refry it in the morning. But remember, bacteria love to grow on food, so this only works when it's really cold outside.

Bagels: Bagels fried in butter and topped with cheese—or summer sausage, or peanut butter.

Instant soup: Eat with the bread or biscuits you baked before going to bed, grilled in your frying pan.

Instant breakfast drinks: These powdered drinks are widely available at supermarkets. They don't fend off hunger and weakness for very long, but they can give you a start. Try mixing them with hot water.

COLD CEREALS

Cold cereal can be a nutritious, high-fiber start to a backcountry day. Some of my favorites are Grape-Nuts, Shredded Wheat, granola, and, sometimes, Raisin Bran. They can be mixed with fruit, dry milk, and water for a quick jump-start in the morning.

Variations: Mix the dry milk thoroughly into the cereal before adding the water. It prevents clumping. Mix two cereals together for variety. Some people like to eat their cold cereal hot. They just pour hot water on the top and eat away. Pick cereals that can be used in other ways, such as baking. Grape-Nuts, for instance, makes a great quick crust if you don't have graham crackers.

BARB'S GRANOLA (Make at Home)
SERVES 3-4

5 cups oatmeal
$\frac{1}{2}$ cup raw cashews
1 cup almonds
1 cup sesame seeds
1 cup unsweetened coconut
1 cup wheat flour or soy flour
1 cup non-instant powdered milk
1 cup wheat germ
1 cup raisins
1 cup honey
1 cup vegetable oil

Combine all dry ingredients. Mix honey and oil together. Blend dry with wet ingredients. Put on two baking trays. Bake at 325°F for 10 minutes. Cool and package.

Thanks to Barb Harper, Gunnison, Colorado, and Lori Patin, Parlin, Colorado

BACKCOUNTRY PAN-FRIED GRANOLA

SERVES 3-4

3-4 tablespoons margarine
$1/2$ cup brown sugar
3 cups oatmeal
$1/2$-1 cup nuts, chopped into bits
$1/2$-1 cup raisins

Melt margarine in frying pan. Add sugar and stir aggressively until it melts. (Be careful—it likes to burn. Try tipping the pan on edge and removing it from flame if sugar starts to burn.) Add all remaining ingredients and fry until brown.

Variations: Add 2 tablespoons of peanut butter and serve as a trail snack late in the trip after everyone has gobbled the gorp.

HOT CEREALS

Although hot cereals have a bad name in many circles, they really can be a warm, tasty way to start the morning, and they are quick. Many people are turned off by their appearance and name. Stop calling them gruel, mush, and bloatmeal, and you may have an easier time choking them down. Call them oatmeal, Cream of Wheat, cream of rice, and other more appealing appellations.

PORRIDGE WITH A TWIST

SERVES 2

1 cup oats (non-instant)
$1/4$ cup dry milk
$1/4$ cup raisins
$1/4$ cup dried chopped apples (or any fruit)
Dash salt (optional)
2 cups water
1 glob margarine
Sugar to taste
$1/2$ teaspoon cinnamon
$1/4$ cup chopped nuts

Bring oatmeal, dry milk, fruit, salt, and water to a boil. Simmer, stirring frequently, until porridge is the desired consistency. Top with margarine, sugar, cinnamon, and nuts. Takes about 10 minutes once water boils.

Variations: Substitute ¼ cup Grape-Nuts or Shredded Wheat for ¼ cup of the oatmeal. It gives it a different texture.

Popular Variations on the Theme

Cream of Wheat: Substitute 2 cups Cream of Wheat for oatmeal. Follow directions for Porridge with a Twist.

Breakfast bulgur / rice / grits: Substitute any of the preceding grains for oatmeal and follow the directions for Porridge with a Twist. Mixing different types together is always a hit. These take a little longer to cook.

Cornmeal pudding: Substitute 1 cup of cornmeal and 4 cups of water for the 1 cup of oatmeal and 2 cups of water in Porridge with a Twist. Proceed with the remaining directions.

BREAKFAST COUSCOUS SPECIAL
SERVES 4

2 tablespoons powdered milk
4 tablespoons of water
4 cups water
¼ teaspoon salt
3 tablespoons brown sugar (or honey)
¼ cup margarine
¼ cup dried fruit chopped into little pieces
2 cups couscous
½ to 1 teaspoon cinnamon
¼ cup sunflower seeds or nuts

Mix powdered milk with 4 tablespoons of water and set aside. Bring water to a boil with salt, sugar, margarine, and fruit in it. Add couscous and the powdered milk mixture and stir. Cover and simmer for 5 to 10 minutes, with only an occasional stir. When the water disappears and the mix looks fluffy, add the cinnamon and seeds/nuts.

BREAKFAST BULGUR SPECIAL
SERVES 2

2 tablespoons powdered milk
4 tablespoons water
2 cups water
$1/4$ teaspoon salt
2 tablespoons brown sugar (or honey)
2 tablespoons margarine
$1/4$ cup dried fruit chopped into little pieces
1 cup bulgur
$1/2$ teaspoon cinnamon or nutmeg
$1/4$ cup sunflower seeds or nuts

Mix powdered milk with 4 tablespoons of water and set aside. Bring water to a boil with salt, sugar, margarine, and fruit in it. Add bulgur and powdered milk mixture and stir. Cover and simmer for 5 to 10 minutes, with only an occasional stir. When the water disappears and the mix looks fluffy, add the cinnamon and seeds—and, yes, this is very much like the Breakfast Couscous Special recipe (page 60).

Variations: Add and stir in 1 teaspoon of vanilla and about 2 tablespoons of peanut butter just before serving.

SWEET RICE
SERVES 1

2 tablespoons powdered milk
$1/2$ cup hot water
$1/2$ tablespoon margarine
$1/2$ tablespoon brown sugar (or honey)
Cinnamon, just a dash
1 cup cooked rice (this could be a leftover but better if hot)
2 tablespoons raisins and/or nuts

Dissolve the milk in the hot water and add the margarine, sugar, and cinnamon. Pour the hot mixture over the bowl of rice and raisins and/or nuts, stir, and consume.

INSTANT HOT CEREAL

Instant cereals—oatmeal, Cream of Wheat or rice, Malt-O-Meal, and so forth—usually require equal amounts of hot water and cereal. Boil water, add cereal, simmer 1 minute, and set aside. Add desired amounts of sugar, fruit, nuts, and spices.

EGGS FOR BREAKFAST

Fresh eggs will keep for a couple of weeks without refrigeration if they are not cracked. Backpacking without breaking them is almost impossible (unless you buy one of those plastic egg cases), but I've had some luck carrying them on paddling trips if they're carefully packed and used early. Most of the outdoor food companies package either powdered or freeze-dried egg breakfasts. Having tried most of these, I can testify that they actually do work. Because the portions are small, I prefer to combine them with other ingredients (e.g., potatoes, rice) rather than eat them separately. Egg powder can also be purchased in bulk so you can add your own spices and choose your own portions. I sometimes carry egg powder, but use it mostly for baking. Don't try to use freeze-dried eggs in baking. They don't work.

SCRAMBLED EGGS

SERVES 2

1/2 cup egg powder
1/4 cup dry milk
1 cup water
Margarine
Spices

Mix all ingredients thoroughly. Scramble in margarine. Add spices to taste.

ELAINE'S IMPOSSIBLE QUICHE

SERVES 2

½ cup egg powder

¼ cup dry milk

¾ cup Essential Batter Mix (see Backcountry Baking) or commercial
    mix

½ cup water

1–2 cups filling (hydrated veggies or meat)

1 cup shredded cheese

Spices to taste

Mix together egg powder, dry milk, Essential Batter Mix, and water.
Spread filling in the bottom of fry-bake pan, cover with sliced cheese,
and add mixture. Stove-top bake for 20 to 30 minutes.

Variations: Place the filling and the mixture on top of a
piecrust (see Backcountry Baking).

Thanks to Elaine Dube, Kennebunk, Maine

POTATOES FOR BREAKFAST

ESSENTIAL HASH BROWNS

SERVES 2–3

1⅓ cups water

2 cups dried hash browns

3 tablespoons margarine

Chili powder, garlic powder, and pepper to taste

1 cup shredded cheese

Combine water, dried hash browns, and margarine in a nonstick skillet.
Cook uncovered until all the water has been absorbed and bottom is
brown. Flip with a spatula. Add spices and cheese. Cover until cheese
has melted and the bottom is brown. Don't stir these; they will turn to
mush and the bottom won't brown.

SCRAMBLED POTATOES AND EGGS

SERVES 2-3

1¹/₃ cups water
2 cups dried hash browns
¹/₂ cup egg powder
¹/₄ cup dry milk
1 cup water
3-4 tablespoons margarine
Garlic, chili powder, black pepper to taste
1 cup shredded cheese

Follow Essential Hash Browns recipe (page 63). While hash browns are hydrating in frying pan, mix egg powder and dry milk with 1 cup water. As hydrated hash browns begin to fry, mix in eggs, add spices, and scramble. More margarine may be needed. Pull off heat, top with cheese, and cover. When cheese is melted, serve.

Variations: Carry one of the many scrambled egg or omelet mixes available through outdoor food companies. Substitute mix for egg mixture and spices. This works well with rice, too.

BROCK'S BEANS AND BROWNS

SERVES 4

2 cups dried hash browns and 4 cups hot water
1 cup instant refried beans and 1 cup hot water
¹/₄ cup egg powder
2 tablespoons dry milk
¹/₂ cup water
¹/₄ cup flour
2 tablespoons margarine
1¹/₂ cups shredded cheese
Garlic powder, chili powder, black pepper, and cayenne to taste

Rehydrate hash browns and beans separately. Mix the egg powder, milk, water, and flour together and blend this mixture into the hydrated potatoes. Then pour it into the fry-bake pan atop the melted margarine. Position sliced cheese over the potatoes and top with beans/spice mixture. Stove-top bake 20 minutes, or until done. Eggs must cook and cheese must melt. If you're in a rush, this recipe works well if you merely roll the crisped hash browns, cheese, and beans into a tortilla.

Variations: Crisp the hash browns before baking. Serve with hot sauce, tortillas, sprouts, and sour cream.

Thanks to Mark Stivers, Lander, Wyoming, and Kate Bartlett, Elaine Doll, Brett LeCompte, and Steve Mital of the Deer Hill School, Mancos, Colorado

HASH BROWN FRITTERCAKES

SERVES 2

1 cup hash browns
1–2 teaspoons dried onion
3 tablespoons (heaping) powdered milk
2 tablespoons flour
3 tablespoons powdered egg
Pepper, just a dash
1 teaspoon salt

Bring a pot of water to the boiling point. Put hash browns and onions in another pot, cover with about 1 inch of hot water, and allow about 15 minutes of rehydration. If they're sort of firm, that's about right. Mix together all the dry ingredients (and you'll need a bowl for this). Drain water from the hash browns and onions; save it. Add 6 tablespoons of that water gradually to the dry ingredients, mixing it well. Add this mixture to the hash browns. Drop large spoonfuls of the final mixture into a hot, greased pan. Flatten each cake. Cook about 3 minutes on a side, or until each cake is golden brown.

Variations: Serve with syrup, cheese, or hot sauce.

MARBLE MOUNTAIN MORNING CAKES

MAKES 4-6 CAKES

1 pound dehydrated hash browns
1/8 cup whole-wheat flour
1/8 cup cornmeal
1/4 pound cheese
Raspberry jelly or preserves

Cover potatoes with about 6 to 8 cups of boiling water. Set aside to rehydrate (about 10 minutes). Be careful not to oversoak the potatoes or else they'll get soggy. Drain potatoes, saving a little water in the bottom. Add flour and cornmeal to mixture until you have a stiff batter. Form and flatten a cake in an oiled frying pan. Cook at medium-high heat, flipping when one side browns. After you flip, put a slice of cheese on the cake and add the lid onto the pan to melt the cheese.

Variations: Serve topped with raspberry jelly syrup.

Thanks to Michael Hock, Santa Fe, New Mexico

PANCAKES

ESSENTIAL PANCAKES

SERVES 2-4

2 cups Essential Batter Mix (see Backcountry Baking, page 129)
1/4 cup egg powder (optional)
1 tablespoon sugar (optional)
About 2 1/4 cups water

Remember to adjust batter for the altitude (see Backcountry Baking, page 130). Slowly mix water into the dry ingredients until batter pours easily off spoon. If it's too thin, add more flour. Pour batter into bottom of a heated, oiled frying pan. Cook over medium heat until bubbles form on the top of the cake. Flip and cook until cake is golden brown and sounds hollow when tapped.

Variations: Substitute buttermilk powder for milk powder in the Essential Batter Mix, or add chopped nuts to the batter.

GRANOLA PANCAKES

SERVES 2-4

1½ cups Essential Batter Mix (see Backcountry Baking page 127)
½ cup granola
¼ cup egg powder (optional)
About 2 cups water

Follow directions for Essential Pancakes.

APPLE PANCAKES

SERVES 2-4

2 cups Essential Batter Mix (see Backcountry Baking, page 129)
1 package hot apple cider mix
1 package instant applesauce
¼ cup egg powder (optional)
About 2¼ cups water

Follow directions for Essential Pancakes.

Variations: Add ½ cup of hydrated dried apple pieces to batter.

WILD AND HOTCAKES

SERVES 2-4

2 cups Essential Batter Mix (see Backcountry Baking, page 129)
1 cup wild berries
2 tablespoons sugar
2–4 tablespoons egg powder (optional)
About 2 cups water

Follow the directions for Essential Pancakes.

Variations: Serve with Pick Your Own Syrup (from later in this chapter).

CORN GRIDDLE CAKES

SERVES 2-4

1½ cups cornmeal
½ cup whole-wheat flour
2 teaspoons baking powder
1 tablespoon sugar
⅓ cup dry milk
About 2 cups water
2 tablespoons oil

Slowly mix the water and oil into the dry ingredients. Cook as described in Essential Pancakes recipe.

Variations: Rehydrate 1 cup of dried corn and add it to the batter before cooking.

BLOATMEAL PANCAKES

SERVES 2-4

1 cup oatmeal
2 tablespoons oil
About 2 cups water
⅓ cup dry milk
½ cup flour
2 teaspoons baking powder
1 tablespoon sugar (optional)
¼ cup egg powder (optional)

Combine oatmeal, oil, and water in pan and let stand for 5 to 10 minutes to soften oats. Stir in the dry ingredients. Flip-bake as described under Essential Pancakes. (Style points are awarded to anyone who utilizes oatmeal in anything but gruel!)

CHOCOLATE LOVER'S PANCAKES

SERVES 2-4

2 cups Essential Batter Mix (see Backcountry Baking, page 129)
$1/4$ cup egg powder (optional)
$1/4$ cup cocoa or $1/2$ cup hot chocolate mix
Chocolate or carob chips, handful
About $2 1/4$ cups water

Follow the directions for Essential Pancakes.

HEALTH CAKES

SERVES 2-4

$2/3$ cup whole-wheat flour
$1/3$ cup white flour
$1/4$ cup oatmeal or cornmeal
2 tablespoons wheat germ or bran
1 tablespoon sugar
2 teaspoons baking powder
2 tablespoons egg powder
4 tablespoons buttermilk powder
1 tablespoon oil
About $1 1/2$ cups water

Mix all dry ingredients. Slowly add oil and water. Cook as described in Essential Pancakes.

PANCAKE TOPPINGS

Quick Toppings
- Brown sugar and margarine
- Jelly
- Instant applesauce
- Peanut butter

CINNAMON BUTTER

1/2 cup sugar

1/2 teaspoon cinnamon

1/4 cup margarine

HONEY BUTTER

1/4 cup margarine

1/8 cup honey

BASIC SYRUP

1/2 cup sugar

1/4 cup water

1/4 cup margarine

1 teaspoon of vanilla or a dash of cinnamon (optional)

JELL-O SYRUP

1 cup water

2 tablespoons brown sugar

3 tablespoons margarine

1/4 cup un-gelled Jell-O (a fruit flavor is best)

To make the syrups, simmer the ingredients in small pan until sugar is dissolved and keep warm. Remember: Sugar likes to burn.

PICK YOUR OWN SYRUP

2 cups wild berries

1/2 cup sugar

Water

Pick the berry of your choice, or any edible berry you can find. Simmer berries with sugar, smashing as you stir. Add water to desired consistency. Some berries require more sugar than others. For example, currants aren't very sweet, while grouse whortleberries are very sweet. Add a little flour as a thickener if you need it.

Tip: It's important to be able to distinguish good berries from bad berries.

HONEY SYRUP

1 cup honey

1 teaspoon vanilla

2 tablespoons water

2 tablespoons margarine

$1/2$ cup shredded coconut

Heat all ingredients to desired consistency.

APPLE SYRUP

$1/2$ cup sugar

$1/2$ cup water

1 package hot apple cider mix

Heat all ingredients to desired consistency.

JELLY SYRUP

$1/2$ cup jelly

3 tablespoons margarine

Heat all ingredients to desired consistency.

THE EYE-OPENER SYRUP ★

2 cups strong coffee

$1/2$ cup sugar

Boil coffee continuously. Add sugar a spoonful at a time and stir. Boil until almost a syrup. It will thicken as it cools down. Pour over your pancakes for the best darn syrup you'll ever have outside of New England.

Thanks to David Tomco, Glastonbury, Connecticut

BREAKFAST BREADS

Don't put more than 2 to 2½ cups of batter into a 9- to 10-inch fry-bake pan because it will rise up and stick to the lid. Adjust recipes for altitude (see Backcountry Baking, page 130).

SIN-A-MON BISCUITS

SERVES 2-4

2 cups Essential Batter Mix or any commercially available mix
½ cup dry milk
½ cup oats (or leftover oatmeal)
½ cup brown sugar
2 teaspoons cinnamon
1 handful raisins
¾ cup water

Combine dry ingredients and mix with water. Fold gently until mixed. Bake in an oiled, heated, covered skillet until brown on one side. Flip and bake until brown.

Thanks to J. Scott McGee, Richmond, Oregon

PSEUDOSCONES

SERVES 2-4

1½ cups Essential Batter Mix (see Backcountry Baking)
½ cup flour
½ cup raisins
¼ cup brown sugar
2 tablespoons egg powder (optional)
1 teaspoon ground ginger
½ teaspoon cinnamon
¼ teaspoon nutmeg
About ¾ cup water

Mix all ingredients into a stiff dough. Press into the bottom of a greased frying pan. Cut dough with a spatula into 6 to 12 triangles. Stove-top bake.

Variations: Serve with cinnamon sugar or orange fruit crystals sprinkled on the top.

FRUITY FRITTERS

SERVES 2-4

1½ cups Essential Batter Mix (see Backcountry Baking, page 129)

2 tablespoons egg powder (optional)

¾ cup water

1 tablespoon sugar

1 cup dried chopped apples (or whatever)

½ teaspoon cinnamon or nutmeg

Rehydrate apples. Combine all ingredients. Drop by spoonfuls into a hot frying pan. Fry in oil until crispy brown.

ESSENTIAL COFFEE CAKE

SERVES 4

2 cups Essential Batter Mix (see Backcountry Baking, page 129)

4–8 tablespoons sugar

2 tablespoons egg powder

½ teaspoon salt

2 tablespoons oil or melted margarine

1 cup water

Mix all dry ingredients in a pan. Add the wet ingredients slowly until most of the lumps are gone. Scrape the batter into an oiled fry-bake pan. Cover the batter with one of the toppings below (or your own) and stove-top bake for 20 to 30 minutes.

Variations: Add 1 package of sour cream mix to the dry ingredients and 1 teaspoon of vanilla to the wet. Top with the topping (see below), but use pecans as the nut.

Topping

½ cup brown sugar

1–2 teaspoons cinnamon

2 tablespoons melted margarine

½ cup nuts (walnuts or almonds are good)

2 tablespoons oatmeal (or flour)

Mix all ingredients in a small pan or bowl and spread as best you can on top of the cake prior to baking it.

WILD MORNING COFFEE CAKE

SERVES 4

Follow Essential Coffee Cake recipe for batter.

Variations: Substitute dry buttermilk for dry milk in Essential Batter Mix.

Topping

2 cups berries (anything nonpoisonous will do)

1 cup dry milk

$\frac{1}{4}$–$\frac{1}{3}$ cup sugar (currants need a lot of sugar)

Mix all ingredients together. Spoon on top of cake and stove-top bake.

MORNING STREUSEL ᵭᵭᵭ

SERVES 2-3

Batter

1$\frac{1}{2}$ cups flour

2 teaspoons baking powder

$\frac{1}{4}$ teaspoon salt

$\frac{1}{2}$ cup sugar

4 tablespoons margarine

2 tablespoons egg powder

2 tablespoons dry buttermilk or milk

$\frac{3}{4}$ cup water

Combine all dry ingredients and then mix in the wet ones slowly. Pour half of mixture into an oiled fry-bake pan. Sprinkle with half of filling (see below). Add other half of batter and filling. Stove-top bake for 20 to 30 minutes or until done.

Filling

2 tablespoons flour

2 teaspoons cinnamon

$\frac{1}{2}$ cup brown sugar

2 tablespoons melted margarine

$\frac{1}{2}$ cup chopped nuts

Mix together in a bowl and set aside until needed.

YEAST CINNAMON SPIRAL ♦♦♦

SERVES 2-3

Make Essential Yeast Bread (see Backcountry Baking, page 139).

Filling

2 tablespoons flour

2 teaspoons cinnamon

$\frac{1}{2}$ cup brown sugar

2 tablespoons melted margarine

$\frac{1}{2}$ cup chopped nuts

Using your water bottle, roll dough into a thin rectangle on top of a plastic bag (more hygienic) or your sleeping pad (less hygienic). Cover the rectangle with the filling, leaving about an inch around the edges. Roll dough into a tight tube and seal-pinch edges closed. If edges won't seal, dab a little water on them. Coil the dough into a spiral starting in the center of your fry-bake pan and working outward. If dough doesn't fill pan completely, press it firmly into the bottom until it does. Stove-top bake until done, about 30 minutes. If you're in a rush you can flip-bake (see Backcountry Baking, page 128), but the end product is denser.

Variations: Cut rolled tube into 1- to 2-inch rounds and stove-top bake circles flat for cinnamon rolls (see Backcountry Baking, page 140).

Munchables

MUNCHABLE OPTIONS

Munchables—some people refer to them as lunchables, or just plain lunches—should total about 20 percent of your total food weight. Supermarkets, health food stores, and outdoor food companies provide a wide enough variety of these items to please almost anyone. Below you'll find listed some of my favorites in terms of taste and durability.

Breads and Crackers
Bagels, tortillas, pita bread, pilot biscuits, Melba toast, bagel chips, rye crisps, or any hardy cracker. Un-hardy crackers usually end up as dust in a plastic bag after a few days of being tossed around.

Trail Mixes
Trail mixes have come a long way since the birth of "good old raisins and peanuts," whenever that was (and who knows if that's really what "gorp" stands for anyway?). Now you can find a very wide variety of mixtures. The point is to come up with something that keeps well, tastes good, and provides an energy boost. Buy trail mixes if you're in a rush, or build your own if you're picky about the contents. And remember that chocolate (as in chips) melts in a hot food bag.

Meat, Cheese, and Peanut Butter
These items are usually represented in the 13 percent of your total weight earmarked as "high-calorie." They make great munchables, especially on cool-weather trips. The harder cheeses (Cheddar, Swiss, Colby, Edam, Gouda) last longer without spoiling. If you leave the cheese vacuum-packed until you're ready to eat, it won't mold. Many summer sausages and pepperoni need no refrigeration until the casing is broken, and even then, they last a long time. Buy them in small packages and plan to share them at one lunch or dinner. Peanut butter is high-calorie but has no cholesterol. It's not as versatile as meat or cheese, but it's good for variety. Peanut butter is also good in soups, sauces, and breads.

Dried Fruits and Nuts

Carry them separately or toss them into trail mixes. They are high-calorie for their weight.

Fresh Fruits and Vegetables

Hardy fruits and vegetables—such as apples and carrots—make great snacks, but they're not light. On a long trip, it's nice to have a few along.

Candy and Granola Bars

As mentioned, chocolate melts in the heat, even in a Snickers Bar. Hard candies are occasionally nice to have in your pocket, especially for energy snacks on the go. On supermarket shelves, you will, of course, find almost endless choices in "granola bars."

Cookies

Fruit bars: They're high-calorie but low-fat, and if you crush them it doesn't matter . . . they just clump together. Whatever you like, try to pick cookies that won't immediately turn to rubble if you stuff your sleeping bag onto them. If you discover small crumbs, use it to make a no-bake pie, or dump the crumbs into a pudding.

Jerky

Jerked meat has been in packs for hundreds, maybe thousands, of years. Although it's hard to find, salmon jerky is excellent. Jerky can also be hydrated and added to meals. You can make your own, and that's described later in this chapter, page 84.

Energy Bars and Drinks

They're low-fat and a nice boost for the next few miles. In case you missed it, see page 22.

MUNCHABLES TO MAKE IN THE BACKCOUNTRY

It doesn't seem to matter how many munchables you bring with you, they will be gone before the end of your trip. Don't berate your companions for eating more than their share of the trail mix. Impress them with your ability to take the bits and pieces of the remaining stores and turn them into tasty treats.

SCOOBY-SNACKS

Follow the Essential Pan Biscuits recipe (see Backcountry Baking, page 131). Sweeten the biscuits with sugar and raisins or add some nuts. Leftover crumbs of cookies or graham crackers combine nicely. Top them with cheese, peanut butter, or margarine, or eat them alone.

Thanks to Dan Robison, Block Island, Rhode Island

Hot Lunches

Instant soups and instant potatoes make a quick hot lunch if you can spare the time to boil water. Ramen noodles only take 3 minutes once the water has boiled. This is an especially nice break on a cold, windy day.

Featured Elsewhere

Backcountry Pan-Fried Granola (see Breakfasts, page 59), along with Pan Biscuits, Sweet Breads, and Cakes (see Backcountry Baking, page 127), can become lunch. Pancakes left over from breakfast will still be good at lunchtime—especially good if you smear peanut butter on them.

MUNCHABLES TO MAKE AT HOME

After cooking any of the bars described below, cool them thoroughly in the refrigerator, then cut them and freeze them until packing time. If you don't cool and freeze them, they tend to break apart and get eaten at home!

SOLO BARS

SERVES 4-6

6 eggs
1 pound brown sugar
1 pound white sugar
$1/2$ teaspoon vanilla extract
4 teaspoons baking soda
$1/2$ pound butter

1 1/2 pounds crunchy peanut butter
9 cups oatmeal
1 pound chocolate chips
1/2 pound raisins
Sunflower seeds to taste
1 cup shredded coconut (keeps the bars moist)

Mix in order given. Bake on two cookie sheets at 350°F until done. Sides will pull away and become golden brown. Don't overcook or they will become hard and crispy instead of thick and chewy.

Thanks to Ruthe Hubbell, Conway, New Hampshire

FRUIT BARS
SERVES 3- 4

1/2 cup dried apricots
1/2 cup raisins
1/3 cup orange juice
1 1/2 cups flour
1/2 teaspoon baking powder
1/2 teaspoon salt
1/2 teaspoon cinnamon
1/2 cup butter
1/2 cup brown sugar
2 eggs
1 cup chopped walnuts
1 cup diced candied fruit

Glaze
1 cup powdered sugar
1 tablespoon hot water
1 1/2 teaspoons melted butter
1/4 cup finely diced candied fruit

Cut apricots into small pieces and combine with raisins and orange juice. Sift together flour, baking powder, salt, and cinnamon and set aside. Cream together butter and brown sugar. Beat in 2 eggs. Stir in fruit mixture and flour mixture. Stir in walnuts and candied fruit. Spread in a 9 x 13-inch pan and bake at 375°F until done. Cool and spread with the glaze.

DEEP IN THE CONGO BARS

SERVES 3-4

2½ teaspoons baking powder
2¾ cups flour
½ teaspoon salt
⅔ cup shortening or butter
1 pound dark brown sugar
3 eggs
½ pound chocolate chips
1 cup chopped walnuts or pecans

Mix baking powder, flour, and salt. Melt shortening and add brown sugar. Allow it to cool slightly and add eggs. Beat well. Add dry ingredients. Stir in chocolate chips and nuts. Bake at 350°F for 25 to 30 minutes.

SEVEN SUMMITS BARS

SERVES 3-4

½ stick butter
1 cup graham-cracker crumbs
1 cup shredded coconut
2 cups mixed chocolate and butterscotch chips
1 can sweetened condensed milk
¾ cup oatmeal
1 cup chopped walnuts

Layer in a 9 x 13-inch pan in the order listed and bake at 350°F for 20 minutes. Cool thoroughly, cut into bars, and freeze them right away or else they'll disappear.

SPLIT-LEVEL RUINS (Ruins Your Appetite)

SERVES 2-3

1 cup chocolate chips
3 ounces cream cheese
$1/3$ cup evaporated milk
$1/2$ cup chopped walnuts
2 tablespoons sesame seeds
$1/2$ teaspoon almond extract
$1^1/2$ cups flour
$1/2$ teaspoon baking powder
$1/4$ teaspoon salt
$3/4$ cup sugar
$1/2$ cup soft margarine
1 egg
$1/2$ cup oatmeal

Melt together chocolate, cream cheese, and milk over low heat. Stir constantly. Remove from heat and stir in walnuts, sesame seeds, and almond extract. Combine remaining ingredients and press them into the bottom of an oiled baking pan (8 x 11-inch). Pour chocolate mixture on the top and spread evenly. Sprinkle with oatmeal. Bake at 375ºF until done, about 20 minutes. Cool.

QUEST BREAD

SERVES 4-6

4 cups whole-wheat flour
$1/3$ cup wheat germ
$3/4$ cup brown sugar
$1/3$ cup oil
$1/4$ cup molasses
4 tablespoons dry milk
$1^1/2$ teaspoons salt
$1^1/2$ teaspoons baking powder
$1/4$ cup sunflower seeds
1 cup water

Combine all ingredients and mix thoroughly. Bake in an oiled 8 x 8-inch pan at 300ºF for approximately 1 hour. Cool, cut into squares, and put in a plastic bag. Make sure bread is cool and dry when you package it. This bread will last for weeks without growing mold.

NUTTY TREATS

Nuts are high in calories and a great source of protein. Unfortunately, they are also a great source of fat. But it's mostly monounsaturated fat (except in coconut—that's why it's so moist and tasty), and they have no cholesterol. Mix nuts into snacks for a nutritional boost.

SPICED NUTS

SERVES 2

2 cups unsalted dry-roasted nuts
1-2 tablespoons hot sesame oil
1-2 tablespoons garlic tamari (or soy sauce and 1/8 teaspoon garlic powder)
$1/2$ teaspoon cayenne

Mix all ingredients together in a bowl. Spread them on a baking sheet and bake at 350ºF for 30 minutes. Stir them two or three times while baking. Allow nuts to cool and then package them in a plastic container.

GOOP BALLS (OR JUST GOOP)

SERVES 2

$1/2$ cup granola
$1/2$ cup dry milk
$1/4$ cup brown sugar
$1/4$ cup raisins
$1/2$ cup chopped nuts
About 1 cup peanut butter

Mix granola, milk, sugar, raisins, and nuts in a bowl or pan. Add enough peanut butter to make the mixture stiff but not crumbly. Roll into "golf balls" and store chilled. You can also mix this in a plastic bag and eat it by the spoonful for lunch.

Variations: Roll balls in shredded coconut before serving. Add chocolate chips instead of nuts.

NUBBLES (NUTS AND NIBBLES)

SERVES 3-4

⅓ cup margarine

1½ tablespoons Worcestershire sauce

1 teaspoon onion powder

½–1 teaspoon garlic powder

1 teaspoon celery flakes

4–5 cups dry cereal (Crispix, Fruit Wheats, Rice/Wheat/
	Corn Chex, etc.)

1 cup unsalted pretzels, broken into bits

2 cups unsalted dry-roasted nuts

Heat margarine, Worcestershire, and spices. Add to cereal-pretzel mixture and mix. Add nuts and stir. Bake at 300ºF on a baking sheet for 10 minutes.

Variations: Okay, add chocolate bits after the mixture cools.

MA'S SUGARY PEANUTS

SERVES 3-4

2 cups sugar

1 cup water

4 cups raw, shelled peanuts

Mix sugar and water in a large frying pan. Add peanuts and bring to a boil. Simmer for 15 to 20 minutes until the liquid crystallizes on the nuts. Spread on a baking sheet and bake at 325ºF for 15 minutes.

Variations: Add a teaspoon of flavoring: vanilla, chocolate, or the like.

Thanks to Eris Mozingo Tilton, Putney, Georgia

JERKY

HOMEMADE JERKY

SERVES 3-4

2 pounds meat (very lean beef, elk, deer, salmon, etc.)
1/2 cup soy sauce or tamari
1/2 cup Worcestershire sauce
1/2 teaspoon garlic powder or crushed garlic
1 teaspoon meat tenderizer
Optional: salt, onion salt, pepper, oregano, basil, thyme, marjoram, or whatever

Partially freeze the meat so it's easier to slice into strips no more than 1/2 inch thick—even thinner is better. Trim away any visible fat. The higher the quality of the meat, the higher the quality of the jerky. Mix the wet ingredients with garlic and meat tenderizer to make the marinade. Gently rub the meat with the desired spices, but use at least a little salt and pepper. Soak the meat in the marinade, in the refrigerator, for at least 24 hours. Drain and then dry the meat with a paper towel. Place the strips evenly on an oven rack, not touching each other, and turn the oven on to about 150°F. The meat will drip, so you might be happier later if you spread a layer of foil on the bottom of the oven. Leave the door of the oven slightly open for better circulation. You'll have black, nasty-looking, excellent-tasting jerky in about 7 or 8 hours—maybe less if you sliced the meat really thin.

Sauces

· · · · · · · · · · · ·

Grains, pasta, and potatoes are just, well, carbohydrates without sauce. Sauce is like a pinch of salt on an egg, salsa on tortilla chips, frosting on a cake—or, for the analogically challenged, sauce is necessary. Who, for instance, can stomach a lot of couscous or bulgur without something being added—such as a sauce! You know that carbohydrates power you around the backcountry, but it's the sauces that make them tasty meals, turning food into an event. All it takes is a little forethought, a few extra ounces in your backpack, and about 5 more minutes.

Although mixing and matching is allowed, even encouraged—hey, who knows what will appeal to your taste buds—white (cream) sauces are generally preferred on pastas, grains, and rehydrated vegetables; red (tomato) sauces and green (pesto) sauces on pasta; and brown sauces (called "gravy" by some) on potatoes and vegetables. Specialty sauces, such as those flavored with curry or peanut butter (see below), go extremely well on rice, couscous, and bulgur.

JUST ADD WATER ... MAYBE

No time (or heart) for from-scratch sauce making? Try an off-the-shelf package of premixed, powdered sauce. You can get a great brown gravy from Knorr or Schilling by adding a cup of water to the powder, bringing the slurry to a boil, and simmering for a couple of minutes.

For a premixed white sauce, you'll need to be sure you've packed some milk—preferably Milkman or any brand that reconstitutes easily without clumping. To get Alfredo, an especially rich cream sauce, from a package, you'll need to pack a little butter or margarine in addition to the powdered milk. The pesto sauces require a splash of oil. The basic rule of packing before a trip is simple: Read the back of the package first.

FROM-SCRATCH SAUCES

With a couple of pioneering efforts on the sauce-cooking frontier, you will soon be amazing your friends, and yourself, by preparing sauces from scratch. All you need is a few extra ingredients in the food bag and a well-stocked spice kit. A huge hunk of the fun is varying the nonessential ingredients to create personal sauces.

BASIC CREAM SAUCE

MAKES ABOUT 1 CUP

	Thin	Medium	Thick
Milk	1 cup	1 cup	1 cup
(4 tablespoons dry milk and 1 cup water)			
Flour	1 tablespoon	2 tablespoons	3 tablespoons
Margarine	1 tablespoon	2 tablespoons	3 tablespoons

As you can see, you can vary the measurements quite a bit and still get cream sauce, so don't worry about it too much if you don't have a measuring device. Melt margarine in bottom of pan over low heat; add flour, stirring constantly to prevent burning, until mixture is as smooth as possible. Add reconstituted milk, slowly stirring constantly to prevent burning. Keep stirring over low heat until it is thick enough. This usually takes about 5 minutes. Take it off the heat and add salt and pepper to taste.

CHEESE SAUCE

1 cup Basic Cream Sauce
1/2–1 cup of your favorite cheese

Make the Basic Cream Sauce first; then, cut the cheese into small bits and add it at the end, with the pot off the burner. Remember: Cheese loves to burn.

MUSTARD CHEESE SAUCE

1 cup Basic Cream Sauce
1/2 cup cheese
1/4 teaspoon garlic powder
1/4 teaspoon mustard powder (or 1 tablespoon mustard)
Dash of cayenne or Tabasco

ALFREDO SAUCE

1 cup Basic Cream Sauce

1/2 cup Parmesan cheese

1/2 teaspoon basil or dill

1/4 teaspoon garlic

Salt and pepper to taste

BROWN GRAVY

1 cup Basic Cream Sauce

1 teaspoon onion flakes

1/4 teaspoon garlic powder

1-2 tablespoons soy sauce or tamari

Add a beef or chicken bouillon cube instead of the soy sauce for a "meat" option. Don't do both or it will be too salty. These sauces are great on pan biscuits for breakfast.

TOMATO CREAM SAUCE

1 cup Basic Cream Sauce

2 tablespoons tomato base

1/2 teaspoon garlic powder

1 teaspoon basil

Variations: Use 2 cups of instant tomato soup instead of base and spices. Serve on pasta.

ASIAN TOMATO SAUCE

1 cup Basic Cream Sauce

2 tablespoons tomato base

1/4 teaspoon ground ginger

1 tablespoon onion flakes

Soy sauce or tamari to your liking

Serve on bulgur or rice.

PEANUT BUTTER SAUCES

PEANUT BUTTER GRAVY

MAKES ABOUT 1½ CUPS

1 cup hot water
½ cup peanut butter (crunchy is better)
¼ teaspoon garlic powder
2 tablespoons vinegar (optional)
3 tablespoons dry milk (optional)
1½ tablespoons soy sauce
Cayenne

Heat water; remove from burner and add other ingredients. Reheat carefully if need arises. Peanut butter easily scorches your pan. This gravy is excellent on spaghetti noodles or, really, any pasta.

HOT SESAME-PEANUT SAUCE

SERVES 2

1 cup hot water
½ cup peanut butter (crunchy is better)
2 tablespoons vinegar (optional)
3 teaspoons hot sesame oil
1½ teaspoons soy sauce or tamari
1 teaspoon onion flakes
½ teaspoon crushed hot red pepper

Heat water; remove from burner and add other ingredients. Excellent served hot or cold over noodles.

OTHER SAUCES

CURRY SAUCE

SERVES 2

1 tablespoon oil
1 tablespoon flour
2 teaspoons onion flakes
$1^1/_2$–2 teaspoons curry powder
$^1/_2$ teaspoon salt
1 teaspoon brown sugar
1 cup water
$^1/_4$ cup dried chopped apples
$^1/_4$ cup raisins

Heat oil and flour over low heat, stirring constantly, until the mixture is smooth. Add spices, sugar, water, and fruit. Bring to a boil and simmer until apples are tender. Serve over lentils, rice, bulgur, or couscous.

ITALIAN TOMATO SAUCE

SERVES 2

$1^1/_2$–2 cups water (more for thinner sauce)
Optional: dried tomatoes, mushrooms, peppers, etc.
$^1/_2$ cup tomato powder
1 tablespoon onion flakes
$^1/_2$ tablespoon parsley
$^1/_2$ teaspoon basil or oregano
$^1/_2$ tablespoon oil
$^1/_4$ teaspoon garlic powder

Bring water and any dehydrated vegetables you are using to a boil. Add the rest of the ingredients and simmer over low heat, stirring frequently, until you are satisfied with the flavoring and consistency. This is a great sauce for pasta, lasagna, and pizza.

MEXICAN SAUCE

SERVES 2

1 cup hot water (more for thinner sauce)
2 tablespoons dried red and green peppers (optional)
Dried tomato (optional)
1 tablespoon oil
2–3 tablespoons tomato powder
1 tablespoon onion flakes
$1/2$–1 teaspoon chili powder
$1/2$ teaspoon cumin
$1/2$ teaspoon basil or oregano
$1/4$ teaspoon garlic powder
1 tablespoon cornmeal or flour
Black pepper

Rehydrate vegetables in hot water. Heat oil, seasonings, and cornmeal or flour in bottom of pan. Combine all ingredients and simmer, stirring frequently, for 5 to 10 minutes. You'll like this on beans, rice, bulgur, or pizza.

Soups

Soups are great pick-me-ups before meals and a wonderful lunch on a cold day with breads or snacks. You can make soups quickly with the ingredients you carry in your pack, or there are lots of quick soups available at your local store or outdoor shop. You can stock up on instant soups at the grocery store. They are fast, inexpensive (though salty), and make great flavorings when added to grains and potatoes. Soups are also a great way to get rid of leftovers or to use up bits and pieces of food at the end of a trip.

ESSENTIAL BROTH

SERVES 2

6 cups water
2–3 bouillon cubes or 2–3 packages instant soup
¼ cup margarine
1–2 cups filler: grains, pasta, potatoes, vegetable, cheese, etc.
Spices, such as pepper or curry, to taste

Boil the water and add bouillon or instant soup. Be careful: This is salty. Add solid ingredients and spices (to taste). Simmer until done.

Popular Mixes

Chicken soup: Chicken bouillon, dried vegetables, noodles or rice, and curry powder.

Cream of chicken: 2 packages instant creamy chicken vegetable soup, rice, black pepper, and thickener.

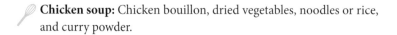
Tomato: Tomato base, rice, black pepper, oregano, garlic powder, milk, and thickener.

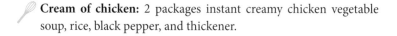
Tomato beef: Tomato powder and beef or vegetable bouillon, dried vegetables, noodles, black pepper, basil, and garlic powder.

Chowder: Vegetable bouillon, dried corn and potatoes, black pepper, basil, garlic, milk, and thickener.

Cream of broccoli: 2 packages instant cream of broccoli soup, dried potatoes, and black pepper.

Lentil soup: Lentils, tomato base, vegetable bouillon, onion flakes, garlic powder, cumin, chili powder, and black pepper.

Miso soup: Cup of miso soup, dried tofu, noodles, onion flakes, garlic powder, and black pepper.

DUMPLINGS

SERVES 2

1 cup Essential Batter Mix (see Backcountry Baking, page 129)
About 1/3 cup water

Mix dry and wet ingredients. Drop batter by spoonfuls onto the top of the bubbling soup. Simmer uncovered until the dumplings are done, about 10 minutes.

Variations: Add herbs or cheese to your dumpling batter.

ESSENTIAL CREAMY SOUP

SERVES 2-3

6 cups water
2-3 bouillon cubes or 2-3 packages instant soup
Spices of your choosing
1-2 cups filler: grains, pasta, potatoes, vegetables, etc.
1/4 cup flour or potato flakes, buds, or pearls (thickeners)
1/2-1 cup dry milk
1/4 cup margarine
Cheese (optional)

Bring water to boil; then add bouillon, spices, and filler(s). Simmer until fillers are tender. Mix thickener into a paste with a small bit of water. Slowly add the paste to the soup, stirring constantly, until thick. Add milk, margarine, and cheese last.

SPICY BEAN AND PASTA SOUP ▲▲▲

SERVES 3-4

2 cups pasta (a white one, like shells or elbows)
4 cups water
2 tablespoons dried green and/or red peppers
1 tablespoon dried onion
2 bouillon cubes (or broth packets)
2 tablespoons margarine
2 cups dehydrated black-bean flakes or dehydrated refried beans
Black pepper, garlic, and chili powder to taste
1 cup grated cheese (Cheddar or Monterey Jack)
Hot sauce or salsa

Cook pasta, drain, and set aside. In another pot, bring water, vegetables, bouillon, and margarine to a boil. Add beans and stir. Add spices to taste. Turn the heat down and simmer until the beans are tender. Add a little more water if it looks thick. Add the pasta. Once served, individual eaters can add cheese and hot sauce or salsa to taste. If it ends up being too thick, spread it on tortillas.

Entrees

Entree is the French word for "entrance." Technically it refers to a dish served prior to the main dish, but I use it, as many Americans do, in reference to the primary food at the end of the day.

BASIC GRAINS

A native grain of Asia, **rice** is the staple food for over half the folks in the world. There are many different types of rice sold in the United States. In terms of shapes, long-grain rice grains are approximately four times longer than they are wide and cook up very fluffy; medium-grain rice is softer and tends to cook up more tender; and short-grain rice is the stickiest.

Brown rice is the whole, unpolished rice grain with only the husk and a bit of bran removed. White rice has been husked and polished, with bran and germ removed. Brown rice takes about twice as long to cook as white rice and has a nuttier, chewier flavor. Precooked or instant rice is the most expensive, the most processed, and the least nourishing, but you can cook with instant rice in situations where you need to save fuel. Brown and white rice are available at the local supermarket in instant and non-instant forms.

Wild rice is not really rice but the seed of a water grass native to the northern Great Lakes. It's very nutritious and a great way to add style points to any meal, in addition to being relatively expensive.

Bulgur is the "rice" of the Middle East. It is really not rice either, but cracked wheat that has been parboiled (steamed and dried) and cracked into small bits. You see it commonly at supermarkets these days, but it can be readily found in bulk at health food stores and co-ops. Bulgur has a nutty flavor. It is great mixed with rice or in any recipe that calls for rice. It cooks faster than rice. People who call bulgur "vulgar" have not been introduced to it correctly.

Couscous is the bulgur of North Africa. It's finely cracked wheat or millet that has been parboiled and refined. It cooks very quickly.

Other grains that are available for a change of pace include: millet (takes a lot of time and water to cook), barley (available in quick-cooking form), kasha or buckwheat groats (an eastern European grain with a nutlike flavor), and corn grits (which can be hard to get outside of the South).

These days there are many companies from which to buy prepackaged grain mixtures of different flavors right at the supermarket. Several companies market meals prepared specifically for outdoor travelers. Many of these options are tasty, but they tend to be expensive and, depending on the brand you pick, can have many additives, especially salt. Unless you are traveling where time and ease of cooking are more of an issue than money and flavor, you will probably prefer to cook your grain dishes from scratch. But you can throw a commercial mix or two in the food bag for a change of pace, or at the end of a long day. If you buy commercial mixes, make sure you get at least a serving and a half per person. Ready-made mixes tend to overestimate the number of people they will serve.

ESSENTIAL GRAIN
YIELDS ABOUT 2½–3 CUPS; SERVES 2

1 cup grain
2 cups water (for wild rice, millet, or barley, use 3 cups)

Wait for the water to boil to add the grain. (It's not required, but it makes the grain less sticky.) Simmer with pot covered so water does not evaporate before the grain is soft. Do not stir grain unless you like it sticky and clumped together. To prevent burning, tip the pot to the side periodically as the water is absorbed to assure there is a small amount of water in the bottom. If the water is gone and the grain is still crunchy, it is acceptable to add more water, preferably hot, but it's not required. Bulgur, couscous, and kasha take about 15 to 20 minutes. White rice will cook about twice as fast as brown rice (30 minutes versus 1 hour). If you prefer brown rice or barley, I suggest buying the quick-cooking style, especially if you are traveling above 10,000 feet. It can take a lot of fuel at higher elevations.

Serving Suggestions for Basic Grains
A quick way to make basic grains more interesting is to cook them with one or two instant soups. Cream of chicken, creamy tomato, and cream of mushroom are consistent favorites. You can serve grains with a Curry or Mexican Sauce (see Sauces). You can cook grains and then fry

them with nuts, herbs, spices, and even a bit of leftover pasta. You can cook grains, add cream sauce, top with nuts, cheese, and bread crumbs, and bake. Mixing grains together is a treat as well, but remember that some take longer to cook than others. Dried vegetables improve the appearance and sometimes the flavor of your grain dishes.

CREAMY SEED PILAF

SERVES 2-3

1 cup rice or bulgur
2 cups water
1 bouillon cube
1 cup Basic Cream Sauce (see Sauces)
1/3 cup Parmesan cheese
1/3 cup sunflower seeds
Salt and pepper to taste

Cook rice with bouillon cube and water. Set aside. Prepare Basic Cream Sauce, adding cheese and seeds last. Season to taste.

Variations: Include 1/3 cup of orzo pasta and 1/2 cup of dried mushrooms in the original cooking.

SPANISH RICE

SERVES 2-3

1 cup rice
2 cups water
1-2 tablespoons onion flakes
1/3 cup dried red and green peppers
1 cup dried tomatoes
1 bouillon cube
2 cups instant tomato soup
1 tablespoon oil
1/2 teaspoon garlic powder
1/2 teaspoon basil
1/2 teaspoon oregano
1/2 teaspoon chili powder
Black pepper and cayenne to taste
1/2-1 cup grated Cheddar

Cook rice, water, onion flakes, dried peppers, dried tomatoes, bouillon cube, and instant soup. Place oil in frying pan. Add rice mixture and spices, including black pepper and cayenne to taste. Fry to desired crispiness, top with cheese, cover and set aside to allow cheese to melt.

Variations: Great with bulgur instead of rice. Use fresh onions and garlic. Serve with tortillas and sour cream dip.

QUICK CURRIED RICE
SERVES 3–4

3 cups water
1 cup rice
1 vegetable bouillon cube
1 cup dried apples, raisins, apricots, cut into small bits
2 tablespoons dried red and green peppers
1 tablespoon onion flakes
1 teaspoon curry powder
$\frac{1}{2}$ cup cashews and/or peanuts
$\frac{1}{3}$ cup shredded coconut (optional)

Bring water, rice, and bouillon cube to a boil. Simmer. When water is half absorbed, add fruit, peppers, and spices. Simmer until done. Mix in nuts, cover with coconut, and serve.

Variations: Use couscous instead of rice. When couscous, fruit, and spices are done, fry in oil with nuts. Sprinkle with coconut and serve with chapatis (see Backcountry Baking, page 135).

SIMPLE FRIED RICE
SERVES 2–3

Rice
Margarine
Spices

After cooking a pot of rice as described in Essential Grain recipe, melt margarine in a frying pan, stir in the rice, and add spices—such as salt, pepper, garlic, and curry—as desired. Cook until golden brown, usually about 10 to 15 minutes.

GOURMET FRIED RICE ♟♟♟

SERVES 2–3

1 cup rice

2 cups water

2 tablespoons onion flakes

2 tablespoons dried red and green peppers

1 tablespoon oil

4 tablespoons egg powder, 1 tablespoon dry milk, and $\frac{1}{2}$ cup water,
  mixed

2 tablespoons soy sauce

$\frac{1}{4}$ teaspoon garlic powder

Black pepper to taste

Sunflower seeds to taste

Cook rice with water and onion flakes, and any vegetables you wish to include. Put oil in frying pan and scramble reconstituted eggs. Add rice mixture to eggs, along with soy sauce, garlic powder, black pepper, and sunflower seeds, and fry until thoroughly hot.

Variations: Cook 1 package of ramen noodles and fry them with rice. Use garlic tamari instead of soy sauce. Add $\frac{1}{2}$ cup of dried mushrooms and/or $\frac{1}{2}$ cup of dried peas and carrots. Top with cashews.

MEXICAN RICE CASSEROLE
SERVES 3-4

1 cup rice or grits
About 3 cups water
1 cup freeze-dried corn
$1/3$ cup dry milk
1-2 tablespoons onion flakes
$1/2$ teaspoon each chili pepper, salt, and pepper
1-2 cups Cheddar, cut into small bits

Cook rice (or grits), water, corn, milk, and spices. Mix all ingredients and pour into fry-bake pan. Sprinkle the cheese on top, cover, and warm over low heat until cheese melts.

Variations: Serve with tortillas and sour cream dip. Salsa or hot sauce makes a nice addition as well.

QUICK SWEET-AND-SOUR RICE
SERVES 3-4

1 cup hot water
3 ounces dried tofu or chicken (optional)
$1/4$ cup raisins or dried apricots
$1/4$ cup dried pineapple chunks
$1/4$ cup dried red and green peppers
2 cups water
1 cup rice
1 package sweet-and-sour mix
3 tablespoons soy sauce

Pour about 1 cup of hot water over dried tofu/meat, fruit, and peppers. Cook rice with 2 cups water. Add sweet-and-sour mix and soy sauce to fruit and vegetable mix. Return to a boil. Pour over rice. Mix and serve.

Variations: Serve with almonds.

SLOW SWEET-AND-SOUR RICE

SERVES 3-4

2½ cups water
1 cup rice
1 teaspoon salt
½ cup raisins
½ cup other dried fruit, chopped
2 tablespoons dried red and green peppers
½ cup nuts and seeds
¼ teaspoon black pepper
2 tablespoons margarine

Sauce

¼ cup water
4 tablespoons vinegar
3 tablespoons soy sauce
3-5 tablespoons brown sugar

Put water, rice, salt, fruit, and peppers into a fry-bake pan and cook, covered, until rice is done. If excess water exists, pour it off carefully. Add nuts, seeds, and pepper and fry in margarine for 5 to 10 minutes. For the sauce, mix the ingredients in a separate pot or bowl and stir into cooked rice. Cover again, and simmer for a few minutes.

BULGUR-RICE PILAF

SERVES 3-4

1 cup bulgur
1 cup rice
4 cups water
Bouillon cube (choose your flavor)
2 tablespoons dried mixed veggies
1 tablespoon dried onion
3 tablespoons margarine (heaping)
½ cup cubed or grated cheese such as Cheddar or Monterey Jack

Put all the ingredients except the cheese into a pot. Cook, covered, over medium heat, for about 20 minutes. Do not stir very much. When it all looks dry and fluffy, add cheese and scoop into an oiled frying pan. Fry until browned.

RICE AND POTATO PATTIES

SERVES 3-4

3/4 cup water
4 tablespoons dry milk
2 tablespoons margarine
1/2 cup Cheddar or Monterey Jack cheese, cut into small bits
2/3 cup instant potatoes
1 cup cooked rice
Garlic powder, salt, and pepper to taste

Boil ¾ cup water with milk and margarine. Remove from heat, add cheese, instant potatoes, and cooked rice, and set aside for a couple of minutes. Spice to taste, form into patties, and fry in margarine or oil. (Great use for leftover rice. If you cook it with a couple of instant soups, it's even better.)

Variations: Cover with brown gravy and add a few sunflower seeds.

CHICKEN CURRY ♦♦♦

SERVES 4

5-6 cups water
2 ounces freeze-dried chicken
1 package freeze-dried peas
1 envelope Knorr Leek Soup
1 envelope Herb-Ox Instant Chicken Broth
3-4 teaspoons curry powder
1½ cups instant rice
Shredded coconut, cashews, raisins (or dried cranberries)

Bring 5 to 6 cups of water to a boil. Add chicken, peas, leek soup mix, and chicken broth. Set aside to rehydrate (15 to 30 minutes). Add curry powder. Bring back to a boil and add instant rice. Cook 5 to 10 minutes until tender, stirring occasionally. Sprinkle with coconut, cashews, and raisins and serve.

Thanks to Iretta Hunter, Danville, California

CLAUDIA'S FAVORITE COUSCOUS PILAF ⟨⟨⟨

SERVES 4

2 cups water
2 broth packets or 2 bouillon cubes (veggie or chicken both work well)
3 tablespoons dried vegetables
1 cup couscous
3 tablespoons margarine (or butter or olive oil)
1/2 to 3/4 cup finely cubed or grated Cheddar or Monterey Jack cheese

Bring water, broth packets, and veggies to a rolling boil. Add couscous and margarine, and stir well. Reduce heat, cover, and simmer for 10 minutes. Check frequently; it can burn easily. Once the grain looks dry and light, remove it from the heat. Stir in the cheese and cover until the cheese melts.

Variations: Instead of dried vegetables, use 1/2 to 3/4 cup sautéed fresh veggies—onions and garlic, yum! Add the fresh veggies after the cheese has melted.

Thanks to Claudia Pearson, Lander, Wyoming

TABOULI SALAD

SERVES 4

2 cups bulgur
2 1/2 cups boiling water
1 tablespoon dried onion
2-3 tablespoons dried mixed veggies
1 mint tea bag
2 tablespoons parsley flakes
1/2 cup oil
1 teaspoon salt
1/4 to 1/2 teaspoon black pepper
5 tablespoons vinegar (optional)

Put bulgur, 2 cups of the boiling water, onion, and veggies in a pot. Steep tea bag in the other 1/2 cup boiling water for 2 to 3 minutes. Discard tea bag and add minty water to pot. Let it sit for 30 minutes. Add remaining ingredients. Stir well. Allow another 30 minutes of cooling (the salad, not you) before dining.

MEATLESS

VEGETARIAN "MEATBALLS" ♦♦♦

SERVES 2-3

³/₄ cup cornmeal
¹/₂ cup whole wheat flour
¹/₄ cup white flour
6 tablespoons powdered milk
¹/₂ teaspoon garlic
¹/₂ teaspoon salt
1 tablespoon dried onion
1 teaspoon soy sauce
¹/₂–³/₄ cup water
1 tablespoon oil

Mix all the dry ingredients together. Add rehydrated onion, soy sauce, and just enough water to make a stiff dough. Form about two dozen balls, about walnut-size. Heat about 1 tablespoon oil in a frying pan. Add balls and roll them around until they are coated with oil. Cover and cook 20 to 30 minutes, shaking them occasionally to make sure they brown all the way around. Eat them as they are.

Variations: Serve them on pasta. Serve them cold . . . later.

PASTA

Pasta cooks up fairly quickly, and it's filling, readily available in wonderfully different shapes and colors, and can even be tasty if you cook it right. You can buy pasta in ready-made dishes, but these suggestions and recipes will add the delight of cooking to dinner.

ESSENTIAL PASTA RECIPE
SERVES 3-4

6 cups water
1 teaspoon oil (optional)
3 cups pasta
OR
1 part pasta to 2 parts water

Heat water to a rolling boil, then add oil and pasta. Cook pasta until it is tender. The time can vary a lot. Angel-hair pasta and Chinese noodles take a short time (3 to 5 minutes) versus shells and whole-wheat elbows, which take longer (12 to 15 minutes). Fettuccini and spaghetti are somewhere in the middle. Altitude will add to the cooking time, since the water is boiling at a lower temperature. Choose your pastas carefully if you will be traveling above 10,000 feet. Whole-wheat and vegetable pastas require the longest cooking times and often go from still crunchy to glue without ever reaching that "perfect" moment. Important: If you add the pasta before the water boils, you are guaranteed to be left with wallpaper paste instead of dinner. Pasta loves company . . . in other words, test pasta frequently to avoid mushy problems.

Serving Suggestions for Pasta
Any of the cream sauces or peanut butter sauces will combine well with pasta (see Sauces, page 85, for recipes.)

Serving Size for Pasta
A pound of pasta generally satisfies four folks if you're also having soup and bread or dessert. I have met many hardy hikers who can easily consume 8 ounces themselves. On cold, long days of hiking, I, embarrassingly, have downed a half-pound of pasta. But on warm desert nights, a quarter-pound has been plenty. So what's the answer? Play around until you figure it out.

FETTUCCINI ALFREDO

SERVES 3-4

1½-2 cups Alfredo Sauce (see Sauces)
1 pound fettuccini
Parmesan cheese

Make the Alfredo Sauce first and set aside. Cook and drain pasta. Warm the sauce, stirring constantly. Add to pasta and serve with Parmesan cheese.

Variations: Add hydrated vegetables for a primavera touch, or add seafood that you harvested yourself.

ITALIAN SPAGHETTI

SERVES 3-4

1½-2 cups Italian Tomato Sauce (see Sauces, page 85)
1 pound thin spaghetti noodles
Parmesan cheese

Prepare Italian Tomato Sauce. Cook and drain pasta. Warm sauce, add to pasta, and serve with Parmesan cheese.

Variations: Add lentils, falafel balls, summer sausage, or hydrated beef to your sauce (a good and tasty protein boost).

MACARONI AND CHEESE

SERVES 3-4

1½-2 cups Mustard Cheese Sauce (see Sauces, page 85)
2 tablespoons onion flakes
3 cups elbows or shells
¼ cup sunflower seeds

Prepare the Mustard Cheese Sauce first, adding the onion flakes with the other sauce ingredients. Cook and drain pasta. Add warmed sauce and sunflower seeds, and serve. For quick mac-and-cheese, leave about 1 cup of water when draining the noodles, add all ingredients for sauce to the pot, and warm slowly over a low flame.

Variations: Add hydrated peas and tuna for a deluxe tuna casserole. Serve with croutons.

ALPINE SPAGHETTI

SERVE 3-4

1 pound thin spaghetti
4 tablespoons oil
1 cup Parmesan cheese
4-6 teaspoons ground sweet basil
1-2 tablespoons parsley flakes
Garlic powder and pepper to taste

Cook and drain pasta. Add oil and toss, then mix in the remaining ingredients and serve.

Thanks to Kitty Ann and Roger Cox, Pitkin, Colorado

AMERICAN CHOP SUEY

SERVES 3-4

3 cups elbows or shells
1 cup dried ground beef (or any type of hardy sausage, cut into small bits)
1-2 tablespoons onion flakes
$\frac{1}{4}$ cup dried red and green peppers (optional)
2 cups water
Cream of tomato instant soup (2 packages) or 2 cups Tomato Cream
    Sauce (see Sauces, page 87)
Black pepper to taste (optional)

Cook and drain pasta. In a separate pot, add dried ground beef, onion flakes, and dried peppers to 2 cups of water. Bring to a boil, and simmer 5 to 10 minutes to rehydrate the ingredients. Add tomato instant soup (or Tomato Cream Sauce). Mix all ingredients, and serve with black pepper to taste (if you have it).

HOT RED PEPPER PASTA

SERVES 2-4

1 pound linguine or fettuccini
¼ cup olive oil
2 teaspoons minced garlic (or garlic powder to taste)
1 teaspoon crushed red pepper
2 tablespoons parsley flakes

Cook and drain pasta. Heat oil in a pan and sauté garlic. (Skip this step if using garlic powder.) Add cooked pasta and remaining ingredients and toss until pasta is coated. Be careful with the crushed red pepper.

Variations: Top with Parmesan and tamari to taste.

SPAGHETTI A LA CARBONDALE

SERVES 3-4

1 pound thin spaghetti
1 tablespoon onion flakes or 1 small onion
2-4 garlic cloves or ¼-½ teaspoon garlic powder
2-3 tablespoons oil
2 tablespoons parsley flakes
2 teaspoons oregano
2 reconstituted eggs (4 tablespoons egg powder and
   4 tablespoons water)
1 cup small bits of cheese (Swiss is nice here)

Cook and drain spaghetti. In a pan, sauté onion, garlic, oil, and spices until tender. Add all ingredients to cooked spaghetti, stir, and let it sit, covered, for a few minutes so the eggs will cook and cheese will melt.

Variations: Add 1 cup of white wine (pass the bota bag, please) and an 8-ounce can of whole baby clams to the sauce.

MILL VALLEY LINGUINE

SERVES 3–4

1 cup sun-dried tomatoes
$\frac{1}{2}$ cup dried mushrooms
Hot water to rehydrate vegetables
1 pound linguine
2 cups water
$\frac{1}{2}$ cup dry milk
Parmesan cheese
Black pepper to taste

Cut tomatoes and mushrooms into smaller pieces and cover with hot water to rehydrate them. Cook and drain pasta. Add milk and 2 cups water and bring to a boil. Add the vegetables and whatever liquid is left. Simmer for several minutes. Add sauce to pasta. Sprinkle with Parmesan cheese and black pepper to taste.

HOT OR COLD "SZECHWAN" NOODLES

SERVES 4–5

1 pound spaghetti- or linguine-type noodles
$1\frac{1}{2}$ cups Hot Sesame-Peanut Sauce (see Sauces, page 88)

Cook and drain pasta. Prepare Hot Sesame-Peanut Sauce and stir into pasta. If you don't like hot foods or aren't carrying sesame oil, this is also very tasty with Peanut Butter Gravy.

Variations: Top with scallions. For the truly bold of palate, add cayenne.

LISAGNA LASAGNA 🍴🍴🍴

SERVES 3-4

2 cups pasta (elbows, shells spirals, etc.)
½ onion
4 garlic cloves
1 tablespoon oil
½ cup wheat flour
½ cup white flour
2 tablespoons powdered milk
2 tablespoons powdered egg
1 tablespoon baking powder (adjust for the altitude; see Backcountry
    Baking, page 127)
1¼ cups water
1 cup Italian Tomato Sauce (see Sauces, page 89)
¼ pound sliced cheese
Oregano

Cook pasta. In a pan, sauté onion and garlic in oil. Remove from pan. In a separate pan, mix flours, dry milk, egg powder, baking powder, and water. Mixture should be the consistency of pancake batter. Put noodles in the bottom of the fry-bake pan and pour batter over the top. Make sauce, substituting fresh sautéed onion and garlic for recommended dry ingredients. Spread sauce over top of mixture in the pan. Cover with thin slices of cheese. Sprinkle with oregano. Stove-top bake for 20 minutes.

Thanks to Lisa Jaeger of Wyoming, Baja, Chile, and Alaska

SMOKED SALMON PASTA 🍴🍴🍴

SERVES 4

4 garlic cloves
2 shallots
3 tablespoons butter
4 tablespoons dried tomato bits
1 envelope Herb-Ox Instant Chicken Broth
½ cup water
8 ounces dry, smoked salmon
8 ounces angel-hair pasta
¼ cup capers
Parmesan cheese

Peel and chop garlic cloves; place garlic and shallots in butter. Add dried tomato bits, chicken broth, and ½ cup water. Let sit 15 to 20 minutes. Flake salmon into garlic-tomato mix. Cook noodles and drain. Toss noodles, salmon-garlic-tomato mix, and capers. Serve sprinkled with Parmesan cheese.

Thanks to Iretta Hunter, Danville, California

HOT TOFU AND SESAME NOODLES
SERVES 4

½ pound tofu or 3 ounces dried tofu
Hot water
1½ cups Hot Sesame-Peanut Sauce (see Sauces, page 88)
3 packages ramen noodles
⅓ cup sesame seeds
½ cup peanuts or cashews

Soften dried tofu by soaking in hot water for about 10 minutes. Prepare Hot Sesame-Peanut Sauce. Cook and drain ramen (do not use the flavoring packet). Combine all ingredients except peanuts/cashews. Smash these up and sprinkle them on just before serving.

Variations: Garnish with green onions or sprouts.

NOT-JUST-ANOTHER-RAMEN DISH
SERVES 2-3

1 tablespoon dried onion (rehydrate in hot water)
3 tablespoons brown sugar
1 teaspoon garlic
½ teaspoon black pepper
3 tablespoons vinegar
3 tablespoons soy sauce
¾ cup water
Bouillon cube of your choice
2 packages ramen noodles
3 tablespoons oil (generous)
2 tablespoons sunflower seeds
3 tablespoons peanut butter

Rehydrate onion. Mix sugar, garlic, pepper, vinegar, and soy sauce into a broth with about ¾ cup water and the bouillon cube. Cook pasta and drain immediately. Heat oil in a pan and stir in seeds and the rehydrated onion; keep stirring for about 2 minutes. Add the broth and peanut butter to the pan, stir quickly, and remove from heat. Pour the mixture over the noodles and eat.

Variations: Try serving this cold.

PASTA SALAD
SERVES 2-3

2 cups pasta
4 cups water
½ teaspoon salt
1 tablespoon each dried onion, dried peppers, mixed dried veggies

Dressing
1 tablespoon vinegar
¼ cup oil
½ teaspoon garlic powder
½ teaspoon salt
Dash of black pepper
2 tablespoons sunflower seeds

Cook pasta, salt, and vegetables in a pot; as this cooks, mix the ingredients for the dressing together. Drain cooked pasta and veggies, pour on the dressing, and eat.

Variations: Substitute rice, bulgur, or couscous for pasta. Italian seasoning adds a nice touch. Toss on a few almonds, raisins, and/or dried cranberries.

VEGETABLE AND SHRIMP PASTA

SERVES 2-4

1 pound shrimp (fresh, frozen, or canned)

2 garlic cloves or ¼ teaspoon garlic powder

½ cup oil

2 cups water

1 package Knorr Vegetable Soup and Recipe Mix (or equivalent)

1 teaspoon oregano

¼ teaspoon crushed red pepper

8 ounces linguine, cooked and drained

If using fresh shrimp, thaw and then sauté shrimp and garlic in oil until shrimp turn pink (about 5 minutes). Remove them from pan. Add water, soup mix, oregano, and red pepper to frying pan and bring to a boil. Simmer for 5 to 10 minutes. Return shrimp to pan (or add canned shrimp). Warm and spoon over cooked and drained pasta.

Variations: Substitute 1 cup of white wine for 1 cup of water. Works well with clams or mussels as well.

POTATOES

Harvested as early as 6000 BCE by South American Indians, this staple of the Incan Empire and the Irish was brought to the United States in the early eighteenth century. Its popularity soared around the turn of the twentieth century, and then plummeted again in the 1950s. Currently, potatoes are on the upswing, but it's mostly in the french-fried form.

Potatoes are a nutritious, hardy addition to a backcountry menu. Unfortunately, their bulk and weight turn most folks to the dried or flake options. If you can afford the space and need the weight, fresh potatoes will be tastier and healthier. They make a great addition to base camp or waterborne travel where weight is less of a consideration. If nothing else, they make a great first breakfast before you hit the trail.

Dehydrated potato flakes, granules, and hash browns are widely available at supermarkets. Additionally, many companies are marketing dehydrated potato-and-sauce mixes. Watch out for these—many are very high in fat and sodium. If you choose to buy them for the variety or ease of preparation, carefully consult the box for serving-size information. A cup and a half per person is reasonable.

ESSENTIAL INSTANT POTATO FLAKES OR PEARLS
SERVES 1

$^2/_3$ cup hot water
2–3 tablespoons dry milk
1 glob margarine
$^2/_3$ cup potato flakes
Salt and pepper to taste

Heat water, milk, and margarine. Stir in potato flakes until just moist. Let stand for 30 to 60 seconds. Add spices and eat.

Serving Suggestions for Potatoes
Instant potato flakes or pearls are invaluable backcountry menu additions. They are an especially quick breakfast or snack before dinner, can be fried up for any meal, and make a great thickener when you put too much water in your soup. They are not good in coffee, so when you wake up gummy-eyed in the morning, don't mistake them for powdered milk.

Variations: Reconstitute potatoes with a cup of instant soup. Add chunked cheese, garlic, and chili pepper.

POTATO-NUT PATTIES
SERVES 2

2 cups potatoes (follow the above recipe to rehydrate)
2 cups chopped nuts (such as walnuts)
$^1/_3$ cup melted margarine
1 tablespoon onion flakes or chives
1 tablespoon parsley flakes

Mix all ingredients together. Form into patties. Fry in oil over medium heat. You can make them without the nuts, if you prefer.

Variations: Top with cheese, let it melt, and serve.

CHEESY POTATO CASSEROLE

SERVES 2-4

1⅓ cups water
6 ounces dried hash browns or sliced potatoes
1 cup Mustard Cheese Sauce (see Sauces, page 86)

Bring water to a boil. Add potatoes and simmer until tender. Make Mustard Cheese Sauce in fry-bake pan. Add potatoes, mix, and bake for 15 minutes or so.

Variations: Top with chives and sour cream.

THUNDER CHILI

SERVES 3-4

2 cups potato pearls
½ cup vegetarian chili mix (or one small can of chili)
4 cups water
Cheese, such as Cheddar or Monterey Jack (crumbled, grated, or
    finely chopped)

Boil water and add chili mix. Cook for 10 to 15 minutes. Remove from heat and mix in potato pearls (do not toss in all 2 cups at once) until you like the consistency. Add cheese until you are happy with the amount and stir until cheese melts—and eat.

Variations: Serve over rice or on tortillas. Top with salsa or hot sauce.

Cooking the One-Burner Way

GRAPE-NUT SURPRISE (aka POWER-LOAD DINNER)

SERVES 3-4

2 cups potato flakes

2 cups instant refried beans

Black pepper, chili powder, cayenne, garlic powder to taste

1/4 cup margarine

2 cups Grape-Nuts

2 cups Cheddar cheese (sliced thin)

Boil 2 pots of water with 2 cups of water in each. Rehydrate potato flakes and refried beans in separate pots. Mix black pepper, chili powder, cayenne, and garlic powder (to taste) into beans. (Be careful if you bought refried beans that have already been spiced.) Set both aside. Melt margarine in bottom of fry-bake pan. Add two-thirds of the Grape-Nuts until they are saturated with fat. Remove from heat and smash into a crust. Cover crust with a layer of sliced Cheddar. Add a layer of potatoes and a layer of beans. Top with a final layer of cheese and sprinkle with remaining one-third of the Grape-Nuts, garlic powder, and chili powder (to taste). Stove-top bake until the cheese has melted (about 10 to 15 minutes).

Thanks to Shana Tarter and Steve Platz, Lander, Wyoming

SPICY SHEPHERD'S PIE

SERVES 4-6

2 cups hot water

2 cups instant potatoes

1/3 cup dry milk

3 tablespoons margarine

1 bouillon cube or one packet instant soup

2-3 cups boiling water

1 cup freeze-dried corn

2 tablespoons onion flakes

1 1/2-2 cups instant refried bean (or black bean) mix

Salt, pepper, and Tabasco to taste

1 cup cheese, such as Cheddar or Monterey Jack, cut into small bits

Combine 2 cups of hot water with potatoes, milk, margarine, and bouillon cube. Set aside. In the bottom of your fry-bake pan, combine 2 to 3 cups of boiling water with corn, instant-potato mixture, onion flakes, and beans. Simmer until corn is tender and beans are hydrated. Remove from heat. Spread potatoes over beans; add salt, pepper, and Tabasco. Top with cheese. Stove-top bake until hot and cheese melts (about 15 minutes).

Variations: Substitute 1 cup of dried ground beef or sausage for half of the beans. Top with sour cream.

SIMPLE POTATO CURRY

SERVES 2

2 cups dried hash brown potatoes
1⅓ cups water
2–3 tablespoons margarine
1–2 teaspoons curry powder
½ teaspoon garlic powder

Fry all ingredients together until water is absorbed and potatoes are tender.

Variations: Top with sour cream.

BEANS: THE MUSICAL FRUIT

Actually, beans aren't fruit at all. They're all dried seeds from leguminous plants. Each bean (legume) has a characteristic flavor and texture, and all beans are excellent sources of protein when combined with grains, seeds, or small amounts of milk, cheese, or meat. The problem with beans in the backcountry is not the snide remarks from your traveling companions, but the time they take to cook. A pot of legumes can take from 20 minutes (lentils) to more than 3 hours (chickpeas) to soften to the point where they are edible. Don't let this discourage you; just choose carefully.

Lentils and split peas make wonderful backcountry meals, and many beans, such as pintos and black beans, can be purchased in quick-cooking styles. Soaking and pressure-cooking beans can cut down on the cooking time as well. And don't forget that falafel and many vegetarian burgers are also bean by-products. Bean dishes are widely available in prepackaged forms from supermarkets, health food stores, and outdoor retailers. Below are some dishes you can easily throw together yourself.

ESSENTIAL LENTILS
SERVES 2

1 cup lentils
3 cups water
$1/4$ teaspoon salt

Cover lentils with water and bring to a boil. Cover and simmer for 20 to 40 minutes, until tender. Although presoaking is not required, it will cut down on the cooking time. Carry them soaking in a water bottle while you hike or paddle. Top with Curry Sauce (see Sauces, page 89) for a change.

ESSENTIAL INSTANT REFRIED BEANS (OR BLACK BEANS)
SERVES 2

1 cup instant beans
1–2 tablespoons margarine
$3/4$–1 cup boiling water

If you have bean flakes, you can add the margarine and boiling water to beans and set aside while they rehydrate (5 to 10 minutes). At high altitude, or if you have dried, whole beans, some limited simmering may be required. If your beans are not pre-spiced, add salt, pepper, chili powder, and cumin to taste.

Variations: Serve with sour cream and sprouts. Top with cheese and use a tortilla as a spoon.

ESSENTIAL FALAFEL
SERVES 2

1 cup falafel
³/₄ cup water
Oil for frying

Mix falafel with water and let stand until it is sort of firm. Form into thin patties (½ inch) and fry in oil. Don't squish them with the spatula while they're in the pan or they will break apart. This is fragile business.

Serving Suggestions for Beans

Top with a slice of cheese, roll in a tortilla, sprinkle on the Tabasco, and eat. Falafel burgers are also delicious with many of this book's sauces (see Sauces, page 85). It's also good with rice. If the taste of falafel is too strong for you, mix the falafel 50/50 with cornmeal or flour.

Variations: Form the falafel into meatball-size rounds and serve with Italian spaghetti.

LENTIL CHILI
SERVES 3-4

4-5 cups water
1¹/₂ cups lentils
4 tablespoons tomato powder
1-2 tablespoons onion flakes
1 tablespoon chili powder (or more, to taste)
1 teaspoon cumin
1 teaspoon oregano
1 teaspoon garlic powder
2 tablespoons cornmeal
Black and red pepper to taste
Cheddar cheese

Combine water and lentils and bring to a boil. Add all ingredients (except cheese) and simmer until done. Serve and top with cheese chunks.

Variations: Add dried peppers, corn, or tomatoes to the chili. Serve over corn bread.

CURRIED LENTILS

SERVES 3-4

3 cups water
1 cup lentils
1 vegetable bouillon cube
1 cup chopped dried fruit
1-2 tablespoons onion flakes
1-2 teaspoons curry powder
$\frac{1}{2}$ cup sunflower seeds or other suitable nuts
$\frac{1}{3}$ cup shredded coconut (optional)

Bring water, lentils, and bouillon cube to a boil. When water is half absorbed, add fruit and spices. Simmer until lentils are tender. Add sunflower seeds (or nuts) and coconut and serve.

Variations: Use a mixture of lentils and rice, or bulgur and rice.

LENTIL PILAF

SERVES 3-4

$2\frac{1}{2}$-3 cups water
$\frac{1}{2}$ cup lentils
$\frac{1}{2}$ cup rice
1-2 packages instant soup (cream of chicken or tomato work well)
1 cup dried carrots
2 tablespoons margarine
4-6 tablespoons dried red and green peppers
2 tablespoons onion flakes
1 teaspoon cumin
$\frac{1}{2}$ teaspoon basil
$\frac{1}{2}$ teaspoon garlic powder

Boil water, add all ingredients, and simmer until tender.

Variations: After everything is tender, fry the pilaf in margarine. Top it with cheese and nuts. When the cheese has melted, serve.

SWEET-AND-SOUR LENTILS

SERVES 3-4

Hot water (to rehydrate)
1/4 cup dried red and green peppers
1/4 cup dried carrots
1/4 cup raisins
1/4 cup pineapple chunks or chopped apricots
1 cup lentils
3 cups water
1 package sweet-and-sour mix
3 tablespoons soy sauce

Pour hot water over dried fruits and vegetables so they'll rehydrate. Cook lentils. Add sweet-and-sour mix and soy sauce to fruit and vegetable mix, and return to a boil. Pour over lentils, mix, and serve.

Variations: Serve with almonds, or combine with pasta for a larger group.

LENTIL PATTIES

SERVES 3-4

1 tablespoon onion flakes
1/2 teaspoon garlic powder
1 cup lentils
3-4 cups water
1 cup bulgur
1 tablespoon parsley flakes
2 tablespoons oil
1/4 teaspoon black pepper
1/4 cup flour

Combine onions, garlic, lentils, and 3 to 4 cups of water. Simmer for 20 to 25 minutes. Add bulgur, parsley, oil, and pepper. Simmer until tender. Mash and mix in flour. If for some reason the mixture is too thin to form patties, add more flour or cornmeal. Form into patties; crisp in buttered frying pan.

Variations: Serve topped with Hot Sesame-Peanut Sauce (see Sauces, page 88).

ENCHILADA PIE ♦♦♦

SERVES 4

2½–3 cups boiling water
2 cups dried instant refried beans
1 cup dried corn
¼ cup dried red and green peppers
1½ cups Mexican Sauce (see Sauces, page 85)
3 10-inch (or the size of your baking pan) flour tortillas
2 cups cheese, cut into slices
1 package sour cream mix

Add 2½ to 3 cups of boiling water to beans and vegetables to rehydrate. Cover and set aside. Put together the sauce. Pour a third of sauce in the bottom of a deep-dish frying pan. Alternate three layers of tortillas, beans, and cheese. Spread remaining sauce on top. Stove-top bake for 20 to 30 minutes. Top with sour cream and serve.

PIZZA

Pizza is a quick and easy dinner that consistently amazes your friends and, sometimes, even your enemies. All you need is a deep-dish frying pan with a lid and the courage to try. Below you will find some crusts that require varying intensity of commitment, plus some traditional and not-so-traditional toppings.

Bottoms (of the Pizzas)

Note: All of these crust recipes fit a 9- to 10-inch deep-dish pan; each pizza serves 2.

SUPERQUICK CRUST

If you have a low commitment level, for the quickest pizza-like meal, heat your frying pan and one side of a tortilla or pita bread, flip it over, add the toppings and the lid until the cheese melts, and you're eating something sort of like pizza in less than 10 minutes.

QUICK PIZZA CRUST

³/₄ cup Essential Batter Mix (see Backcountry Baking, page 129)
³/₄ cup flour
¹/₂ cup water
1 tablespoon oil

Mix into a stiff dough. Oil bottom of fry-bake pan. Press dough firmly into bottom of pan. For a low commitment level, flip-bake the crust about 10 minutes a side. (Add toppings after the flip!) If you have the time, add toppings and stove-top bake for a much more pizza-like product.

Variations: Add 1 to 2 teaspoons of Italian seasoning to the dough before mixing in the water.

THE "REAL THING" PIZZA CRUST

1 tablespoon dry yeast
1 tablespoon sugar or honey
²/₃– ³/₄ cup lukewarm water
1¹/₂ cups flour
¹/₄ teaspoon salt

Combine yeast, sugar, and water in an insulated mug. When yeast froths to the top, combine slowly with flour and salt, stirring at first and then kneading until the dough is smooth. Put in a warm place to double in size. Knead again until dough is smooth. Press into bottom of oiled pan, add toppings, and stove-top bake about 20 to 30 minutes. (For more help on yeast and baking in general, see Backcountry Baking, page 127.)

Tops (of the Pizzas)

Note: All of these topping recipes fit a 9- to 10-inch deep-dish pan; each pizza serves 2.

TRADITIONAL LID

¾ cup Italian Tomato Sauce (see Sauces, page 89)
Dried veggies of your choice (rehydrated)
1 cup mozzarella cheese
Parmesan cheese

Top the crust of your choice with sauce, rehydrated vegetables, and cheese. Bake by preferred method.

HERB LID

1 cup Cheese Sauce (see Sauces, page 86)
½–1 tablespoon basil, chives, sage, or rosemary (or a combination)

Top the crust of your choice and bake by preferred method.

MEAT LOVER'S LID

1 cup Italian Tomato Sauce
OR
1 cup Tomato Cream Sauce (see Sauces, page 87)
1 cup sliced sausage or pepperoni
1 cup cheese, such as Cheddar, Monterey Jack, or mozzarella, cut into
    small bits

Top the crust of your choice with sauce, meat, and finally, cheese. Bake by preferred method.

VEGETARIAN LID

1 cup Italian Tomato Sauce (see Sauces, page 89)
1–2 cups dried vegetables, rehydrated (peppers and mushrooms
    work well)
1 cup cheese, such as Cheddar, Monterey Jack, or mozzarella, cut
    into small bits

Top the crust of your choice with sauce, rehydrated vegetables, and cheese. Bake by preferred method.

Variations: Substitute cream sauce for the tomato sauce. Sprinkle with sunflower seeds.

TRUSTAFERRIAN LID

1 cup Alfredo Sauce (see Sauces, page 87)
1 cup dried mushrooms, rehydrated
1 cup sun-dried tomatoes
Parmesan cheese and crushed red pepper to taste

Top your crust of choice with sauce, rehydrated mushrooms, and tomatoes. Bake by preferred method. Let folks sprinkle the Parmesan and, especially, the red pepper themselves, according to their preference.

Variations: Top with sprouts.

HOT-TO-TROT LID

1 cup Mexican Sauce (see Sauces, page 90)
1 cup freeze-dried corn
1 cup Cheddar cheese, cut into small bits
Tabasco to taste

Top the crust of your choice with sauce, rehydrated corn, and cheese. (Goes well with Pan Corn Bread—see Backcountry Baking, page 127.) Bake by preferred method.

Variations: Add 1 cup of meat, lentils, or beans to sauce.

FRESH FISH

Let's say, for the sake of a poetic moment, that trout—name your preferred species: rainbows, cutthroats, browns—are rising to dry flies on a splendid mountain lake. You've landed a couple that will just about fit in the pan you're carrying. Dinner awaits.

Clean the fish soon after catching. Slit the abdomen open from vent to chin, slice off the head, and remove the entrails. Scrape out the kidney tissue that lies along the backbone within the body cavity. This stuff comes off easily, using your thumbnail as a tool. Wash what remains of the fish thoroughly in cold water.

If it's a trout, the cleaning is finished. Scaly fish, such as a south Georgia sunfish, will need the scales removed before cooking. Lay a scaly fish on its side and, with the dull side of a knife blade, remove the scales by scraping from tail to neck with brisk little strokes. The sooner after deciding the fish will be eaten that you undertake the scaling operation, the smoother the operation will go.

FRIED FISH

Fish (any species is suitable for frying)
Butter
Flour or cornmeal
Spices: salt, pepper, Mrs. Dash

If the butter is warm enough, rub a bit on the fish first. Sprinkle on the spices. Liberally coat the fish with flour or cornmeal. Obviously, you can fry fish without flour or cornmeal, but they seal in and add to the fish's flavor. Melt a little butter in a pan, and plop in the fish. Watch it carefully. As soon as the flesh is no longer translucent, turn the fish over with a spatula, and continue the careful watching, removing as soon as the flesh lifts easily from the bone. Caution: It is very easy to overcook and, therefore, ruin a fish. Err toward undercooking for the best bet in fried fish.

POACHED FISH

Fish (leaner fish lend themselves better to poaching)
Salt

Thoroughly salt the fish and place it in a pan. Add water to the pan until the fish is barely covered. Put a lid on the pan and bring the water to a boil. Reduce the heat to a simmer and cook until the flesh is flaky, usually about 10 minutes.

Variations: Add onion powder, or (better) onion flakes, or (even better) a chopped onion to the water.

FISH CHOWDER
SERVES 2

1 cup dehydrated hash brown potatoes

1/4 cup onion flakes

1 tablespoon green pepper flakes (if available)

Handful of dried mushrooms, corn, peas, or whatever you have that looks like a vegetable (optional)

Powdered milk (enough to make 1 liter when reconstituted)

Potato Buds

Salt and pepper

Fish, cut into small chunks (fatter fish work better)

Put the hash browns, onion, green pepper flakes, vegetables, and milk in a pot, and mix with enough water to rehydrate the stuff and make a slushy soup. Bring it to a boil, stirring frequently, then add enough Potato Buds to thicken the chowder to the consistency you like. Add more water if it gets too thick. Add salt and pepper to taste. Once the chowder is cooked to your liking, reduce the heat to a light boil and throw in chunks of raw fish. Cook for 5 more minutes. Time it so you don't overcook the fish. Serve hot.

Thanks to Cliff Jacobson, River Falls, Wisconsin

CHEESE

CHEESE BOMBS
SERVES 2

1/2 cup flour

Baking powder, a dash or two

Powdered milk, a couple of pinches

Salt, a little

1/4 cup powdered egg

1 broth packet (or a bouillon cube)

Hard cheese, cut into squares or rectangles

Mix all ingredients together except the cheese. Add water until it reaches the consistency of thick pancake batter. Dip the cheese into the batter and fry the little chunks in hot oil.

Backcountry Baking

Breakfast deep in the backcountry takes on an unappealing familiarity: cold granola, sticky oatmeal, something unidentifiable dumped into lukewarm water in hopes it will dissolve completely before you try to swallow it. But it doesn't have to be that way. How does a fresh-baked cinnamon roll sound—and smell? Served hot, the melting butter dribbles over your fingers. You'll search futilely for descriptors. And the longer the trip, the more you'll appreciate, at any meal, freshly baked changes in diet.

OPTION 1: STOVE-TOP BAKING

The Tools

You will need one deep (1½ to 2 inches) nonstick fry-bake pan with a lid that fits snugly. Your batter or dough should not overfill the pan. Half-full is a good gauge, or the rising that ensues when you bake will cause the batter to overflow, or, minimally, stick to the lid. The lid must fit tightly to ensure that you adequately trap the required amount of heat. If your pan is smaller than this, merely cut the recipes in half and proceed as directed.

The Heat

You will need a source of bottom heat—in this case, a backpacking stove that simmers well. In preparation for stove-top baking, light your chosen stove and adjust it to a simmer. You should be able to hold your hand comfortably about 10 inches above the stove, but still feel your hand being warmed. Too hot is generally more of a problem than too cold.

Equally as important as bottom heat is a source of top heat. Traditionally, this is where you build a small, hot, twiggy fire on top of your lid. The convection dome marketed by Backpacker's Pantry, however, offers a better alternative. Both options will be discussed.

Stove-Top Baking with the Twiggy Fire

Gather a pile of pencil-size (or smaller) twigs. Light your stove and let it run at its lowest heat. Put the baking pan, with secure lid, on the stove, and build a twiggy fire on the lid. Spread the fire out evenly on the lid, and feed it enough wood to keep it burning. It's almost impossible to produce too much heat on the lid. Every 4 to 5 minutes, rotate the pan clockwise to assure even baking on the bottom. Use a couple of sticks to make rotating the pan simple and painless. Total cooking time usually runs 30 to 40 minutes. After 20 to 30 minutes, or if you start to smell a rich aroma, carefully lift off the lid and check the progress, just to be safe. Don't lift the lid too often, or you will keep losing the heat needed to bake the goodie. When the dough is cooked, it has a firm crust and sounds hollow when you thump it. Set the pan off the stove, but continue to burn the twiggy fire on top until nothing is left except a fine ash that can be scattered harmlessly.

Stove-Top Baking with Convection Dome

This item has revolutionized stove-top baking. Follow the directions for baking with a twiggy fire, only skip the twiggies. The convection dome surrounds the fry-bake pan, trapping all the heat around and on top of the pan. You have a lightweight mini oven! Although the twiggy fire works great, the convection dome cuts down on baking time (about 30 percent), as well as the chance of fire. It folds neatly into the pan for travel. Basically, what you're doing is converting your pan into an Outback Oven (see Gear for the Outdoor Kitchen, page 36).

OPTION 2: FLIP-BAKING

Flip-baking is faster. You end up with a still tasty yet denser version of your stove-top baked bread. It is useful if you are in a rush, you forgot your convection dome (heaven forbid), the twiggy supply in the area is low, or the fire danger is high. Merely oil your fry-bake pan, place the dough or batter inside, and flip carefully when it is done on one side. Cook until both sides are toasty and the middle is not gooey. Time per side depends on the thickness of the dough and the heat of the stove. To prevent "black on the outside, goo on the inside," flip-bake over medium heat with the lid in place. I like to flip-bake pancakes, pan biscuits, chapatis, tortillas, johnnycakes, and other things when I'm too hungry to wait.

ESSENTIAL BATTER MIX INFORMATION

The initial Essential Batter Mix ingredients will vary from pancakes to quick breads to piecrust. What will vary is the consistency of the batter and the additional ingredients (the ingredients that make it special). For example, pancake batter needs to be lump-less and pour easily; muffins and cakes need to be thicker but still pour if you encourage the batter; and biscuit dough needs to be just that—dough (sticky, but you can form it into a ball and it stays there). The following recipes will include some ideas about amounts of fluid needed, but the best plan is to add water slowly until the batter reaches the desired consistency.

ESSENTIAL BATTER MIX

SERVES 2-3

2 cups flour
$\frac{1}{3}$-$\frac{1}{2}$ cup dry milk
4 teaspoons baking powder
$\frac{1}{2}$ cup margarine or shortening
$\frac{1}{2}$ teaspoon salt (optional)
Water

How Much Water?

- *For pancake batter*—About 2 cups; batter should run off spoon easily.
- *For cake batter*—About 1½ to 1¾ cups; batter should walk off spoon quickly.
- *For muffin/quick bread batter*—about 1¼ to 1½ cups; batter should drop off spoon into pan, but it's not in a huge rush. This batter is about twice as thick as pancake batter.
- *For biscuit batter*—About ¾ cup; this batter is quite stiff but still sticky. You definitely have to push it off the spoon or press it into a pan. It will not go anywhere by itself.

Important: Altitude Adjustments!

The thing that does seriously affect baking is the altitude at which you are cooking. The higher you go, the less leavening agent (baking powder) you will need. So when making your Essential Batter Mix, either at home or on the trail, think about your altitude and adjust your ingredients appropriately. Also, buy double-acting baking powder. It releases its leavening in two stages so cakes won't rise too fast.

If you do not adjust for the altitude, your baked goods will expand out of your pan, crumble into a small pile, and be otherwise inedible without rolling them into crumb balls or eating them with a spoon.

Baking Powder (use double-acting)

- 0–3,500 feet: Use 4 teaspoons per 2 cups flour.
- 3,500–6,500: Use 3½ teaspoons per 2 cups flour.
- 6,500–8,500: Use 3 teaspoons per 2 cups of flour.
- 8,500–10,000: Use 2½ teaspoons per 2 cups of flour.
- Over 10,000: Use 2 teaspoons and an extra egg (2 tablespoons powdered egg) per 2 cups of flour.

There are more-exact adjustments, but this works. If the recipe calls for a lot of sugar, many people cut it back a tablespoon or two as they gain elevation. I don't usually worry about it, but using too much sugar at the higher altitudes may make your cakes fall by destroying their cell structure.

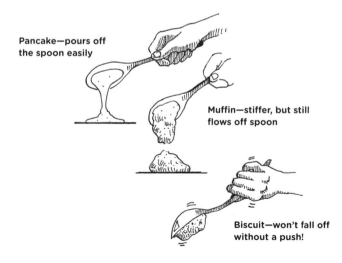

Pancake—pours off the spoon easily

Muffin—stiffer, but still flows off spoon

Biscuit—won't fall off without a push!

COMMERCIAL MIXES AND ALTITUDE

Commercial mixes are prepared for sea level; in fact, most have altitude adjustments on the packaging. Your cake mixes expand like a bad horror movie all over the oven. To combat this dilemma, you must add extra flour to the mixes. Also, add some extra water to compensate for the extra flour and the fact that water evaporates faster at these drier heights. Please don't be overwhelmed. Use the guidelines below to adjust your commercial mixes before baking.

For every 2 cups of mix, add:
- 3,500–6,500 feet: 2 tablespoons each flour and water.
- 6,500–8,500 feet: 3 tablespoons each flour and water.
- 8,500–10,000 feet: 4 tablespoons (¼ cup) each flour and water.
- Above 10,000 feet: 4 tablespoons (¼ cup) each flour and water and an extra egg.

ESSENTIAL PAN BISCUITS
SERVES 2-3

2 cups Essential Batter Mix
³/₄ cup water

Mix wet with dry ingredients. Form into a ball. Knead lightly (about 30 seconds). Pinch off balls of dough and form into patties (½-inch thick) and fry in buttered frying pan a few minutes a side.

Variations: Serve smothered in syrup or gravy (see Breakfasts, page 56, and/or Sauces, page 85).

Popular Variations on the Theme

Buttermilk biscuits: Make the Essential Batter with buttermilk powder and proceed as in Essential Pan Biscuits.

Bacon biscuits: Add ⅓ cup bacon bits to Essential Pan Biscuits and proceed as above.

Cheese and garlic biscuits: Add ½ cup grated cheese and ½ teaspoon garlic powder to Essential Pan Biscuits.

Herb biscuits: Add ½ teaspoon dry mustard, ½ teaspoon sage, and 1¼ teaspoons caraway seeds to Essential Pan Biscuits. Other herbs work well, too.

Sin-a-Mon biscuits: See Breakfasts, page 72.

Pseudoscones: See Breakfasts, page 72.

TRAVELING OAT CAKES

SERVES 3-4

½ cup oil
½ cup sugar
2 tablespoons dry milk
About 1 cup water
2¼ cups white flour
1 cup wheat flour
¾ cup oatmeal
1 teaspoon salt
2 teaspoons baking powder
1 teaspoon cinnamon

Bring oil, sugar, dry milk, and water to a boil. Stir until sugar is dissolved and remove from heat. Combine dry ingredients, add sugary milk mixture, and stir until all ingredients are moist. Shape dough into round biscuits ½ inch thick and 3 inches in diameter, and flip-bake as described in Essential Pan Biscuits.

Variations: Pull these out at lunch and serve with cheese, jam, or peanut butter.

JAM JEWELS ♙♙♙

SERVES 2-3

2 cups Essential Batter Mix
³/₄ cup water
Syrup

Follow mixing directions for Essential Pan Biscuits. Form dough into patties approximately 3 inches in diameter and ¼ inch thick. Drop a spoonful of jelly or thick Berry Syrup in the middle. Fold over and pinch edges tightly shut. If you have trouble sealing dough, dab a little water on the edge. Flip-bake in margarine, or snuggle them into the bottom of your pan and stove-top bake.

QUICK BREADS

SPEEDY BANNOCK (Simple Mountain Bread)

MAKES ONE 10-INCH ROUND

2 cups Essential Batter Mix (¹/₂ white, ¹/₂ wheat works well)
1 cup water

Mix dry with wet ingredients. Place or press in oiled fry-bake pan. Stove-top or flip-bake until done.

Variations: Add cinnamon, sugar, and raisins.

HERB AND CHEESE QUICK BREAD

MAKES ONE 10-INCH ROUND

1 batch Speedy Bannock batter
1 teaspoon garlic powder
1 teaspoon basil or oregano or Italian spices
¹/₄ cup Parmesan or Romano cheese

Combine all ingredients and proceed as in Speedy Bannock recipe.

CORN BREAD
MAKES ONE 10-INCH ROUND

1 cup cornmeal

1 cup flour

$1/2$ teaspoon salt (optional)

1 tablespoon sugar

2 tablespoons egg powder

2 teaspoons baking powder

1 tablespoon oil or melted margarine

$1/4$ cup buttermilk powder

$1^1/_3$ cups water

Combine all ingredients until they are just wet. For traditional johnnycakes, divide the batter into two to three portions and flip-bake in a frying pan. For corn bread, stove-top bake.

Variations: Add 1 cup of hydrated corn and/or 1 cup of cheese bits. For crunchy corn bread, add $1/4$ cup of sunflower seeds to the batter.

HUSH PUPPIES
SERVES 2-3

1 cup cornmeal

$1/2$ cup white flour

1 tablespoon sugar

$2^1/_2$ teaspoons baking powder

2 tablespoons egg powder

1 tablespoon onion flakes

3 tablespoons buttermilk powder

Salt to taste

About $3/4$ cup water

Mix all ingredients together thoroughly. Put a liberal amount of oil into a frying pan. Drop by spoonfuls (or shape into patties) into hot oil and fry until they are brown. These are traditionally deep-fried, but you can get away with a lot less oil by turning them frequently.

CHAPATIS

MAKES 12

2 cups whole-wheat flour
3/4 cup water
1/2 teaspoon salt (optional)
2 tablespoons oil

Mix all ingredients and knead until dough is smooth. Pinch off about 12 small balls of equal size. Pat balls into thin patties between your hands until they are very thin. Drop the flattened dough into a hot frying pan. Cook on one side until brown and then flip. Cook second side. They take about 2 minutes a side.

FLOUR TORTILLAS

MAKES 12

2 cups white flour
1 teaspoon baking powder
1/2 teaspoon salt (optional)
1 1/2 tablespoons shortening or margarine
3/4 cup cold water

Mix dry ingredients and cut in shortening (or margarine) with a spoon—or blend it with your washed hands. Add the water slowly until you have a stiff dough. Divide the dough into 12 balls. Roll them out very thin between two plastic bags. Use your water bottle as a rolling pin. Flip-bake about 2 minutes a side.

QUICK SWEET BREAD

SERVES 2-3

2 cups Essential Batter Mix
1/4-1/2 cup sugar
2 tablespoons egg powder
1 1/2 cups water

Combine dry ingredients and stir in wet. Do not overmix. Pour into oiled fry-bake pan and stove-top bake until done, about 20 to 30 minutes.

Popular Variations on the Theme

Fruit sweet bread: Add 1 cup of chopped dried fruit (apples and raisins work well, but mixed fruit works well, too—or just raisins) and ½ teaspoon of cinnamon to the Quick Sweet Bread recipe above. Rehydrate fruit with hot water before adding it to mixture.

Wild berry bread: Add 1 cup of wild berries and proceed as above.

Oatmeal quick bread: Substitute 1 cup of oats for 1 cup of Basic Batter Mix. Add ½ cup raisins and ½ teaspoon cinnamon.

Coffee cake: See Breakfasts, page 73.

APRICOT BREAD

SERVES 2-3

1¼–1½ cups boiling water
⅔ cup dried, chopped apricots
1½ cups Essential Batter Mix
½ cup Grape-Nuts
½ cup sugar
2 tablespoons egg powder

Pour boiling water over the apricots. Combine all dry ingredients and mix in wet. Add rehydrated apricots. Pour into oiled fry-bake pan and stove-top bake until done, about 20 to 30 minutes.

Variations: Add ½ cup chopped nuts. Pecans are nice.

BACKCOUNTRY CARROT BREAD ♦♦♦

SERVES 2-3

2 cups Essential Batter Mix (or any commercial baking mix)
1/2 cup dry milk
1/2 cup brown sugar
1 teaspoon cinnamon
1 grated carrot
1 handful of raisins
3/4–1 cup water

Combine batter mix, dry milk, sugar, and cinnamon. Gently add carrot, raisins, and water. Mix until all ingredients are wet, and press into the bottom of fry-bake pan. Flip-bake on low heat until done.

Thanks to J. Scott McGee, Redmond, Oregon

PEANUT BUTTER BREAD ♦♦♦

SERVES 2-3

2 cups flour
4 teaspoons baking powder
1/3 cup sugar
1/2 cup dry milk
2 tablespoons egg powder
3/4 cup peanut butter
1 1/3 cups water

Combine all dry ingredients. Cut in peanut butter with two knives or forks until the mixture is crumbly. Add water and mix all ingredients thoroughly. Pour into oiled fry-bake pan and stove-top bake until done, about 30 to 40 minutes.

GRAPE-NUT BREAD ♟♟♟

SERVES 2-3

1¼ cups Grape-Nuts
3 tablespoons margarine
¼ cup brown sugar
2 tablespoons egg powder
¼ cup dry milk
About 1¼ cups water
1½ cups flour
1½ teaspoons baking powder
¼ teaspoon salt
½ teaspoon cinnamon

Sauté the Grape-Nuts in margarine for about 5 minutes. Remove from heat and add sugar. Beat together the egg powder, dry milk, and water. Add the Grape-Nuts. Mix all the remaining dry ingredients and combine with the wet. Stove-top bake in oiled fry-bake pan until done, about 20 to 30 minutes.

YEAST BREADS

Yeast . . . something that sometimes makes breads rise, a source of fear and loathing, certainly not to be considered when packing for the wilderness. Wait a minute . . . why not? Yeast wants to be your friend.

Yeast is a colony of minute fungi, living organisms, sleeping as dried flakes, powder, or cake. Warm water is needed to wake it up, and sugar is required to feed it while it grows. Yeast causes dough to rise by forming tiny pockets of carbon dioxide secondary to the fermentation of the sugar. Water should be very warm but not hot (you should be able to hold your finger in it, but just barely), and the sugar can be white, brown, molasses, honey—whatever you choose.

ESSENTIAL YEAST BREAD
SERVES 2-3

1¼ cups warm water
1 package yeast (1 tablespoon)
2 tablespoons sugar
1 teaspoon salt (optional)
3 cups flour
2 tablespoons oil or melted margarine (optional)

Combine the warm water, yeast, and sugar. (Some people like to add 1 teaspoon of salt and 1 or 2 tablespoons of oil; some people don't.) You can let the yeast begin its life in a pre-warmed plastic, insulated mug to hold the heat. In about 5 to 10 minutes, the mass in the mug starts to bubble out the top; the yeast is fully awake and ready to use. Yeast is fragile during the first few minutes of awakening, and it will die if it gets too cold . . . or too hot. But once it's mixed with flour, it grows strong and hard to kill.

Put about 2 cups of the flour in a pot, and add the activated yeast mixture. I like to mix wheat and white flour, 50/50. Beat the mixture together with a spoon for 3 to 4 minutes, until it becomes a stringy mess. Add more flour slowly, kneading it into the mixture. Kneading can be done in the pot, in a frying pan, on a plastic bag—wherever it's convenient. Keep adding flour and kneading until a non-sticky ball of dough that holds its shape is formed. Total flour used will probably be about 3 cups.

Don't worry too much about your kneading style. You can use the palms of your hands, folding the dough toward you and then turning the ends on top when it starts to get too narrow to comfortably work. Basically, dough likes a firm massage, so come up with your own method.

Plop the kneaded dough in a well-oiled, covered pot and set it in the sun to rise. If it's cold, you can oil the surface of the ball of dough, put it in two plastic bags, and wear it inside your clothing until it rises. For fresh rolls in the morning, whip up the dough ball at night, double-bag it, and sleep with it.

If you're in a hurry, dough doesn't have to rise to be used. The heat of baking will cause some rising. But the more it rises, the lighter and less dense the final product will be.

Before baking, knead the dough again for a few minutes, and place it in a well-oiled fry-bake pan. Stove-top bake, for a lighter yeast bread, or flip-bake, for a denser bread.

Variations: Divide and roll your dough into snakes, then twist, braid, or spiral the snakes around inside your pan. Practice your knots with the snakes and bake them that way. For rolls, pinch off bits of the dough, roll them into balls, and pack them tightly into your fry-bake pan.

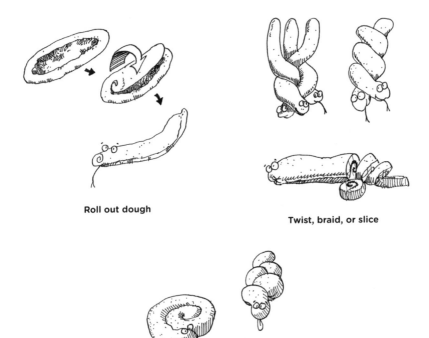

Roll out dough

Twist, braid, or slice

Form spirals or balls

Popular Variations on the Theme

Nutrition boost: Add 2–4 tablespoons egg powder and ½ cup dry milk to dry ingredients. Substitute ½ cup wheat germ or bran for ½ cup flour.

Fruit and nut bread: Add handful of dried chopped fruit and nuts to dough before adding final cup of flour.

Vegetable bread: Add 1 tablespoon hydrated onion flakes, ½ teaspoon garlic powder, ½ tablespoon parsley, and ½ cup rehydrated, smashed-up vegetables. Use a packet of bouillon instead of salt. Add black pepper to taste. A handful of sunflower seeds is nice in this one, too.

Multigrain bread: Substitute ½ cup cooked grain for ½ cup flour. This is a great way to get rid of leftovers.

Chili bread: Add 1 teaspoon chili powder, 1 teaspoon basil, and ¼ teaspoon each of garlic and cayenne. Top with cheese and/or beans.

Raisin oatmeal bread: Substitute ½ cup cooked oatmeal for ½ cup flour. Add ½ cup raisins and ½ teaspoon cinnamon.

SWEET CINNAMON BREAD ♟♟♟

SERVES 2-3

1 Essential Yeast Bread dough
2 teaspoons cinnamon
½ cup brown sugar
Handful of raisins
Handful of nuts

Proceed with Basic Yeast Bread recipe but, before you add the last cup of flour, add the extra ingredients.

Thanks to J. Scott McGee, Redmond, Oregon

GARLIC HERB BREAD ♦♦♦

SERVES 2-3

2 tablespoons herbs (oregano, basil, Italian, parsley, etc.)
2 fresh garlic cloves or 1 teaspoon garlic powder
Melted butter
1 Essential Yeast Bread dough

Sauté garlic and herbs lightly in melted butter. Let cool and add before blending in last cup of flour. Proceed as in Essential Yeast Bread.

Variations: Add ½ cup of Parmesan to dry ingredients. Just before you're ready to bake, press chunks of Swiss cheese into the dough, about 1 inch apart. Stove-top bake.

Thanks to J. Scott McGee, Redmond, Oregon

Desserts

No matter where you find yourself at the end of a day outdoors, it feels (and tastes) good to give yourself a reward: dessert!

NO-COOKING-REQUIRED DESSERTS

PUDDING

SERVES 2

1 instant pudding mix
½ cup dry milk
2 cups cold water

Don't add too much water. You shake the mix in a water bottle (45 seconds) or whisk it (1 to 2 minutes) and then secure it in a stream or snowbank to thicken. It makes a great rich shake or cake topping, too.

Variations: Add leftover rice to pudding.

SNOW SHAKE

SERVES 1

2 tablespoons egg powder
¼ cup dry milk
1 tablespoon sugar
1 teaspoon vanilla
1 cup water

Combine above ingredients thoroughly and add snow until mixture is thick and creamy.

Variations: Leave out the sugar and add 2 to 3 tablespoons hot chocolate, pudding, or cheesecake mix.

SNOW CONES

- Mix fruit-drink crystals or apple cider mix into a syrup. Pour over a mug of snow.
- Sprinkle fruit-flavored gelatin over a mug of snow.
- Mix a mug full of snow with any of the syrups (see Breakfasts, pages 70–71).

Tip: Pick your snow wisely.

LIMITED-COOKING-REQUIRED DESSERTS

CHOCOLATE FONDUE
SERVES 2-4

4 tablespoons margarine
2 cups dry chocolate frosting mix
1 teaspoon instant coffee or cinnamon and cloves to taste
1 tablespoon dry milk
3 tablespoons water

Melt margarine and combine all ingredients. Heat until hot but not boiling. Dip in with sweet bread, cake, graham crackers, vanilla wafers, marshmallows, fruit, or anything else you can find.

ALMOST PEANUT BUTTER CUPS
MAKES ONE 10-INCH ROUND

$1/4$ cup margarine
$3/4$ cup peanut butter (crunchy is better)
$1/2$ pound powdered sugar
$3/4$ cup graham cracker or cookie crumbs
$1 1/2$ cups chocolate chips

Melt margarine and mix in peanut butter, sugar, and crumbs. Press into bottom of fry-bake pan. Melt chocolate chips and pour them over crust. Chill for an hour or so, if you can wait that long.

Thanks to Tilda Musgrove, Live Oak, Florida

NO-BAKE PIE
MAKES ONE 10-INCH PIE

Crust
1/3 cup melted margarine
1 cup graham-cracker crumbs
3 tablespoons sugar

Filling
1 instant pudding mix
1/2 cup dry milk
2 cups water

You can buy Oreo, graham cracker, or ginger-snap crumbs in the baking section of most supermarkets, or just carry the cookies carelessly in your pack for a few days and let the job do itself. Melt margarine and combine it with the crumbs and sugar. If you're using cookie crumbs, leave out the sugar. Press mixture into the bottom of a frying pan. Make pudding in a bowl, or shake it in a water bottle. Pour over crust and set aside to chill.

Favorite Combinations:
- Oreo crumbs and milk chocolate pudding
- Ginger-snap crumbs and tapioca
- Graham-cracker crumbs and banana or coconut pudding

CHEESECAKE OR CHOCOLATE MOUSSE PIE
MAKES ONE 8- TO 10-INCH PIE

These mixes are commercially available packaged with directions and crust, but here are some general guidelines if you buy bulk or lose the directions.

Crust
Mix crumbs with 3 tablespoons melted margarine. Press crumbs firmly into bottom of the pan. We like to sprinkle them on the top of filling for a quick, non-frustrating option.

Filling

Mix filling (about 1 cup) with ½ cup dry milk and about 1½ cups cold water. Beat with whisk or spoon until thick. Place on crust, cover, and set aside to chill.

Variations: Top cheesecake with berry syrup.

MAINE NO-BAKE COOKIES

SERVES 4-6

½ cup margarine

2 tablespoons dry milk

½ cup water

2 cups sugar

3 tablespoons cocoa

3 cups quick oats

½ cup peanut butter

1 cup chopped nuts (optional)

Bring margarine, milk, water, sugar, and cocoa to a boil. Remove from heat and mix in remaining ingredients. Press into bottom of a pan and set aside to cool. Cut and serve.

Variations: While still warm, form the mixture into the shape of moose scat and, later, convince your companions that's what you are really eating. Be careful if you are traveling with small children, or you may find them sampling all kinds of wilderness excrement.

POWERHOUSE NO-BAKE COOKIES

MAKES 10–12 COOKIES

1/2 cup brown sugar

2 tablespoons margarine

1 1/2 tablespoons powdered milk

2 tablespoons water

1/2 cup oatmeal

1/2 cup peanut butter

1/4 cup nuts

2 tablespoons chocolate chips

1/4 teaspoon vanilla

Mix sugar, margarine, milk, and water in a pan. Bring to a boil. Reduce heat and boil for 3 minutes, stirring constantly to prevent scorching. Remove from heat and stir in remaining ingredients. Drop by the spoonful onto a flat surface such as a pan lid. Let them sit for about 10 minutes before eating.

CHEWY FUDGE NO-BAKE COOKIES

MAKES 20–24 COOKIES

1 cup brown sugar

5 tablespoons margarine

1/4 cup cocoa mix

3 tablespoons powdered milk

3 tablespoons water

1 1/2 cups oatmeal

1/4 cup nuts

1/2 teaspoon vanilla

Mix sugar, margarine, cocoa, milk, and water in a pan. Bring to a boil. Reduce heat and boil for 3 minutes, stirring constantly to prevent scorching. Remove from heat and stir in remaining ingredients. Drop by the spoonful onto a flat surface such as a pan lid. Let them sit for about 10 minutes before eating.

ESKIMO NO-BAKE COOKIES

MAKES ABOUT 16 COOKIES

1 cup oatmeal (instant will work)
6 tablespoons margarine
6 tablespoons brown sugar
3 tablespoons cocoa mix
1/2 teaspoon vanilla
1/2 tablespoon water

Mix all the ingredients together. Form the mix into walnut-size balls. Let them sit and chill, if you want to, or just eat them right up.

Variations: Roll the balls in coconut before consuming.

Thanks to National Outdoor Leadership School (NOLS), Lander, Wyoming, for Powerhouse, Fudge, and Eskimo Cookies

CREAMY RICE PUDDING

SERVES 3–4

1 cup instant rice
1 1/2 cups water
2 tablespoons egg powder
1/3 cup dry milk
1/4 cup brown sugar
1/4 cup raisins
1/2 teaspoon cinnamon or nutmeg
1/2 teaspoon vanilla (optional)

Combine all ingredients in a pan. Bring to a boil and simmer until rice and fruit are tender. Stir frequently, as this one likes to scorch. Add more water (preferably hot) if needed.

Variations: Serve for breakfast. Or add 1/4 cup or more hot chocolate for a chocolate dessert.

THE DELIGHT
SERVES 2

2 tortillas
½ tablespoon margarine
½ to 1 cup peanut butter
Chocolate chips (handful)
Brown sugar (handful)
Raisins (handful)
2 fig bars (crumbled)

Smear a tortilla with peanut butter and place it in a buttered frying pan. Sprinkle on chocolate chips and sugar. Heat until the chips and sugar melt. Top with raisins and crumbled fig bars. Cover with second tortilla and fry until crispy. Watch carefully to prevent burning of tortilla!

Variations: Flip the filled tortillas to brown both sides. Add other ingredients you think might work.

Thanks to NOLS Pacific Northwest, Conway, Washington

CRUNCHY CHOCOLATE MESS
SERVES 2

½ cup margarine
½ cup chocolate chips
1 cup granola
Glob of peanut butter

Mix margarine and chocolate chips in a pan and warm over low heat, stirring constantly until it forms a melted ooze. Place the granola in the bottom of a pan. Pour the warm mixture over the granola. Let the mixture cool, smear peanut butter on top, and serve.

BAKING-REQUIRED DESSERTS

GRAHAM-CRACKER SURPRISE

SERVES 4-6

1/2 cup margarine
1/2 cup brown sugar
8 graham crackers or their crumbs
1/2 cup walnuts or pecans

Mix margarine and sugar in a pan, and bring to a boil, stirring constantly. Place the graham crackers in the bottom of your fry-bake pan. Add the nuts to the boiling ooze and pour the mixture over graham crackers. Stove-top bake for about 10 minutes. Let the mixture cool and serve.

COFFEE BARS

SERVES 4-6

1/2 cup brown sugar
1 1/2 cups Essential Batter Mix (see Backcountry Baking, page 129)
1/4 cup oil
2 tablespoons egg powder
3/4-1 cup strong warm coffee
1 teaspoon vanilla (optional)
1 cup chocolate and nut bits

Mix all ingredients and pour into an oiled fry-bake pan. Stove-top bake for about 30 minutes.

Quick and Easy Cakes

Carry a commercial cake and frosting mix. Most 10-inch fry-bake pans will accommodate only half a normal-size cake mix (1½ to 2 cups). Remember to adjust for the altitude by adding flour and water (see Backcountry Baking, page 130).

ESSENTIAL CAKE MIX
MAKES ONE 10-INCH-ROUND CAKE

2 cups flour

3/4 cup sugar

2 1/2 teaspoons baking powder

1/4 cup egg powder (optional)

1/4 cup milk powder

1/3 cup margarine

1/4 teaspoon salt (optional)

1 teaspoon vanilla (optional)

1 1/4–1 1/2 cups water

Mix all dry ingredients and stir in the wet until batter is smooth. Pour into a well-oiled and floured fry-bake pan. Stove-top bake about 20 to 30 minutes.

Popular Variations on the Theme

Chocolate Cake: Add 1/4 cup cocoa, an instant chocolate pudding, or 1/2 cup hot chocolate mix. Add more chocolate for a richer, darker cake.

Chocolate buttermilk cake: Make a chocolate cake (see above) and substitute dry buttermilk for dry milk.

Spice cake: Add 1 teaspoon cinnamon and 1/2 teaspoon each nutmeg, cloves, and allspice. Include 1/4 cup hydrated raisins and 1/4 cup walnuts or pecans.

Applesauce cake: Add 1 package instant applesauce (Backpacker's Pantry), 1 teaspoon cinnamon, 1/2 teaspoon each cloves and allspice, 1/2 cup raisins, and 1/2 cup chopped nuts.

Coconut pudding cake: Add an instant coconut pudding mix and cover with Coconut Hailstorm (see page 153).

DEVIL-MADE-ME-DO-IT CAKE ♨♨♨

SERVES 4-6

½ devil's food cake mix
½ package instant chocolate pudding mix
½ cup dry milk
¼ cup egg powder
1¼ cups water
1 cup chocolate chips (or as many as you can pick out of the trail mix)

Mix all ingredients until smooth. Pour into an oiled and floured fry-bake pan. Stove-top bake for 30 to 40 minutes.

FRUITY UPSIDE-DOWN CAKE ♨♨♨

MAKES ONE 10-INCH ROUND

1–2 cups hot water
1–2 cups dried mixed fruit
3 tablespoons margarine
4–6 tablespoons sugar
1 cup chopped nuts
1 Essential Cake Mix batter (using 1¼ cups water)

Rehydrate fruit with some hot water (1 to 2 cups) in the bottom of your fry-bake pan. Add margarine, sugar, and nuts. Follow recipe for Essential Cake Batter. Pour mixture over the top of the fruit. Stove-top bake until done, 20 to 30 minutes.

Variations: Use apricots and pecans with a chocolate cake. Top with caramel icing.

CRAZY MIXED-UP BOSTON CREAM PIE ♨♨♨

MAKES ONE 10-INCH ROUND

1 Essential Cake Mix batter (using 1¼ cups water)
1 instant vanilla pudding mix
½ cup dry milk and 2 cups cold water
1 cup chocolate chips

Stove-top bake one Essential Cake Mix batter. Prepare one instant vanilla pudding mix and set aside to chill. When cake is done, sprinkle with chocolate chips, cover, and set aside for chips to melt. Cover with pudding and serve.

FROSTINGS, ICINGS, AND A FEW HAILSTORMS

Quick Toppings

- Carry frosting mix; they come in just-add-water varieties.
- Chocolate, carob, or butterscotch chips: After cake is done, scatter chips on the top, cover, and set aside until chips melt. Peppermint patties work great too, but you'll need to spread them after they soften.
- Instant pudding topping: Make pudding first. Set it aside to chill while you bake the cake. Spread it on top of cooled cake.
- Cover cake with one of the syrups or butters (see Breakfasts, pages 70–71).
- Sprinkle cake with powdered sugar or cinnamon sugar.

COCONUT HAILSTORM

ALL OF THE TOPPINGS WILL COVER APPROXIMATELY A 10-INCH ROUND CAKE

1½ cups coconut flakes

⅓ cup brown sugar

⅓ cup soft margarine

2 tablespoons dry milk or buttermilk

½ teaspoon vanilla

¼ cup water

Combine all ingredients, spread over top of warm cake, and cover until melted.

Variations: Build a small twiggy fire on top of the oven to brown coconut.

ESSENTIAL FROSTING I

2 tablespoons flour
1 tablespoon dry milk
¼ cup water
¼ cup sugar
¼ cup margarine
½ teaspoon vanilla

Heat flour, dry milk, and water until very thick. Set aside to cool. Add sugar, margarine, and vanilla. Whip with wire whisk or spoon until thick (a whisk is really useful with this one).

ESSENTIAL FROSTING II

1½ cups powdered sugar
1 tablespoon dry milk
¼ cup soft margarine
½ teaspoon vanilla
2 tablespoons water

Combine dry and then add wet ingredients slowly. It really doesn't take much water, so be careful.

Popular Variations on the Theme

🎩 **Chocolate sauce:** Add 2 tablespoons cocoa or ¼ cup hot chocolate mix.

🎩 **Mocha sauce:** Add 2 tablespoons cocoa and substitute coffee for water.

🎩 **Spice frosting:** Add ½ teaspoon cinnamon and a sprinkle of nutmeg and cloves.

Truly Gourmet Frostings

🍴 **International frosting:** Add ¼ cup of any of the instant International Coffees to Basic Frosting I or II. Café Français is a particular hit.

Thanks to Jennifer Gray Rouillard, Newark, New Jersey

CARAMEL ICING †††

1 cup sugar
2 tablespoons dry milk
⅓ cup water
5 tablespoons soft margarine
1 teaspoon vanilla (optional)

Combine sugar, milk, and water in a pan. Bring to a boil, stirring constantly. Cook until a soft ball starts to form. Remove from heat. Add margarine and vanilla. Beat until creamy. If it's too thick, thin by adding water 1 teaspoon at a time. If it's too thin, add flour.

Variations: Thin out the frosting by adding water. Poke holes in the cake and pour the icing over the top.

RICH FUDGE FROSTING †††

1½ cups sugar
3-4 tablespoons dry milk
¾ cup water
⅓ cup cocoa or ¾ cup hot chocolate mix
2 tablespoons margarine
½ teaspoon vanilla (optional)

Combine sugar, milk, water, and cocoa in a pan. Cook over medium heat, stirring constantly, until mixture comes to a boil. Boil, stirring very occasionally (only to prevent sticking), until mixture thickens and will become syrup when dropped in cold water. (Try a little drop occasionally in your mug.) At this point, remove from heat, add margarine and vanilla, and cool until lukewarm. Beat with spoon until fudge thickens and quickly spread it on cake.

Variations: Double the recipe. Spread in a pan and serve as fudge after it cools.

PEANUT BUTTER FROSTING ♦♦♦

2 tablespoons peanut butter

1½ cups powdered sugar

1 tablespoon dry milk

2–3 tablespoons water

Cream all ingredients together and spread on cooled cake.

CRISPS, COBBLERS, AND PIES

CRISPY FRUIT CRUNCH

SERVES 4-6

2 cups dried fruit (or any type of edible berry is scrumptious)

½ cup raisins

1–2 cups reconstituted orange drink (or use water and sugar as
    another option)

½ cup nut bits

½ cup quick oatmeal

¼ cup flour

¼ cup brown sugar

¼ cup margarine

½ teaspoon cinnamon

Combine fruit or wild berries (use less fluid if using fresh versus dried
fruit or berries) and orange drink in bottom of fry-bake pan. Bring to a
boil and set aside, covered. Combine remaining ingredients and spread
evenly over fruit. Stove-top bake until crisp, about 20 minutes.

WILD CURRANT COTTLESTONE PIE

SERVES 4-6

1 cup flour

½ cup sugar

1½ teaspoons baking powder

3 tablespoons milk powder

¾ cup water

2 tablespoons margarine

2 cups currants (or any other edible berry)

Combine flour, sugar, baking powder, and milk in a pan. Add water and mix until the batter is smooth. Melt margarine in bottom of fry-bake pan. Pour in batter. Pile berries on top. Stove-top bake until done.

Thanks to Tim Lindholm, Boulder, Colorado

APPLE COBBLER
SERVES 4-6

2 cups dried apples
1/4 cup brown sugar
2 tablespoons margarine
1/2 teaspoon cinnamon
1 1/2 cups water
1/2 cup oatmeal (or flour)
1 cup Essential Batter Mix (see Backcountry Baking, page 129)

Combine apples, sugar, margarine, cinnamon, and water in a fry-bake pan. Bring to a boil and simmer until fruit is tender. Meanwhile, mix oatmeal and Essential Batter Mix into a stiff batter. Spoon mixture onto tender fruit and stove-top bake until dough is brown.

ESSENTIAL PIECRUST
MAKES ONE 9- TO 10-INCH CRUST

1 1/3 cups flour
1/3 cup margarine
1 tablespoon dry milk
3-4 tablespoons cold water

Combine all ingredients and work into a ball. Press dough into the bottom and sides of a fry-bake pan.

Variations: Double recipe for double-crust pie.

RAISIN PIE

MAKES ONE 10-INCH PIE

1½ cups raisins

1½ cups water

⅓ cup sugar

2 tablespoons flour

1 cup chopped nuts

1 teaspoon cinnamon

½ teaspoon cloves (optional)

1 Essential Piecrust

Simmer raisins in water until tender. Add sugar and flour and boil for 1 minute. Add nuts and spices. Spoon into pie shell. Stove-top bake until shell is done, about 20 minutes.

APPLE PIE

MAKES ONE 10-INCH PIE

1 Essential Piecrust

Filling

1½ cups chopped dried apples

½ cup raisins

2 cups water

½ cup sugar

2 tablespoons flour

Topping

½ cup brown sugar

1 teaspoon cinnamon

2 tablespoon butter

½ cup chopped nuts

2 tablespoon oatmeal

Simmer apples, raisins, and water until tender. Add sugar and flour and boil 1 minute. Pour into pie shell. Mix all topping ingredients together and crumble onto top of apple mixture. Stove-top bake until crust is done, about 20 minutes.

Coffee and Other Addictions

Hot drinks should be a part of your backcountry diet. They warm you. Most of them energize you. They are a more pleasant way to wait while meals cook than just sitting there. They make you more socially acceptable—or at least there's a chance they will. They hydrate you, to some degree, depending on the drink.

Caffeine opens your eyes, sharpens your mind, lifts your mood, increases endurance, hides tiredness, and hones your senses to a hair-splitting edge. It also makes your hands shake, increases your heart rate, keeps you awake, ups your stomach acid and your need to urinate, and stains your teeth. So what. I can't imagine a backcountry morning (or any morning) without coffee. Coffee, if you're worried, has no connection with heart disease, benign or malignant cancers, or any other illness. If you drink too much caffeine for too long, you'll have withdrawal symptoms—headache, lethargy, anxiety, irritability—when you can't find any. But two or three cups a day are a boon, a blessing, a gift from the gods.

YIPPEE-KI-YAY COWBOY COFFEE

Mini espresso machines and backcountry percolators are nice and unnecessary . . . even though I sometimes use them. All you really need is an old pot and lots of ground coffee beans. For every cup of water in the pot, approximately, put in one heaping tablespoon of coffee, approximately. Always throw in a little extra coffee . . . for the pot. Put the pot on the stove and watch it impatiently. A watched pot never boils, which is why you watch it. Boiled coffee will be bitter. Just as the black water starts to move around under its own power, take it off the stove, cover the pot, and wait a few minutes for the grounds to settle. Pour off a steaming cup while unsuccessfully trying to keep all the grounds in the pot. Later you spit out the grounds that work their way into your mouth. This is a necessary and treasured aspect of cowboy coffee. If you choke a little on the first and last swallow, it's probably just right.

CHEATER'S COFFEE

Several manufacturers—Folgers (folgers.com) is one of them—put ground coffee in a single-serving, tea-style bag. Put the bag in your insulated travel mug and fill the mug with boiling water. Snap on the mug's lid and wait about five minutes while the coffee steeps. It ain't cowboy coffee, but it's better than no coffee. If you tear the bag open—accidentally or on purpose—you still get to spit grounds. And there's always instant coffee, a product sort of similar to real coffee.

Before Starbucks added the name Via to instant coffees, I refused to drink any—no matter what. Via comes in little sticks, one serving per stick, with the words "soluble and microground coffee" on them. They are not bad (starbucks.com).

HOT CHOCOLATE

Some people, surprisingly, prefer the taste of chocolate to the taste of coffee. Save yourself a lot of bother and buy the kind of instant hot chocolate that requires no added milk. A strong cup of hot chocolate provides about as much caffeine as a weak cup of instant coffee. Hot chocolate has plenty of sugar for energy.

Then there are those people who like to mix hot chocolate and coffee. These people are usually indecisive, but the resulting brew is not bad. For the truly lazy, General Foods International Coffees are instant flavored mixes with a very acceptable taste, sort of like premixed hot-chocolate-and-coffee for cheaters.

TEA

As all good residents of the British Isles know, afternoon and evening is the time for tea. Tea is a fine settling-down drink. Many people prefer caffeine-free herbal teas, which settle you down more than teas with caffeine.

Tea Plus is concocted by steeping tea bags (in 6 cups of water if you want tea for 4) and then mixing in your choice of either 3 tablespoons instant lemon drink, 4 tablespoons of instant orange drink, or a packet of instant apple cider. You can also stir in a little sugar for a boost.

OTHER OPTIONS

Flavorful, hydrating energy boosts can be provided by drinking several beverages hot that come in powders and are not usually thought of as a hot drink: Jell-O, Tang Instant Breakfast Drink, apple cider, lemonade. When it comes to hot-drink options, you're limited by only your imagination and your ability to heat water.

APPENDIX

Cups per Pound of Commonly Packed Foods

Food (1 pound)	Measure
Almonds, shelled	3$\frac{1}{2}$ cups
Apples, dried	4–5 cups
Apricots, dried	3$\frac{1}{2}$ cups
Barley, pearled	2 cups
Beans, black, instant	4$\frac{3}{4}$ cups
Biscuit mix	3$\frac{2}{3}$ cups, lightly packed
Bulgur	2$\frac{2}{3}$ cups
Butter	2 cups
Cashews	3$\frac{1}{4}$ cups
Cheese, Parmesan, grated	5$\frac{1}{3}$ cups
Chocolate chips	2$\frac{1}{2}$ cups
Cocoa powder	4 cups
Coconut, dried	4 cups
Cornmeal	3 cups
Couscous	2$\frac{2}{3}$ cups
Cream of Wheat	3 cups
Eggs, dried	4 cups
Falafel, instant	3$\frac{1}{4}$ cups
Farina	3 cups
Flour	4 cups
Fruit drinks	3 cups
Gelatin, flavored	2$\frac{1}{3}$ cups
Grits, dry	3 cups
Honey	1$\frac{1}{2}$ cups
Hot chocolate, instant	4 cups
Hummus, instant powder	4 cups
Lentils	2$\frac{1}{4}$ cups
Macaroni	3$\frac{1}{2}$–4 cups
Nonfat dry milk	4 cups
Noodles, egg	8–9 cups
Oatmeal	5 cups
Peaches, dried	3 cups
Peanut butter	1$\frac{2}{3}$ cups

Peanuts, shelled	3 cups
Peas, dried split	2 1/3 cups
Pecans, shelled	3 cups
Potato flakes	6 cups
Pudding mix	3 cups
Raisins	3 cups, packed
Refried beans, instant powdered	3 1/2 cups
Rice	3 cups
Rice, instant	9 cups
Rice, wild	2 cups
Sesame seeds	4 cups
Sugar, brown	3 cups, firmly packed
Sugar, powdered	4 cups
Sugar, white	2 1/4 cups
Sunflower seeds	3 1/2–4 cups
Tomatoes, dry flakes	2 3/4 cups
Vegetables, dried	5–6 cups
Walnuts	4 cups
Wheat bran	4 cups
Wheat germ	4 cups

Substitutions

1 teaspoon baking powder	equals	1/4 teaspoon baking soda + 1/2 teaspoon cream of tartar
1 tablespoon bouillon	equals	1 bouillon cube
1 cup margarine	equals	7/8 cup vegetable oil
1 teaspoon mustard powder	equals	1 teaspoon mustard, Dijon
1 teaspoon onion powder	equals	1/4 cup onion, fresh minced
1 teaspoon onion, minced dried	equals	1/4 onion, fresh minced
1/3 cup pepper, sweet flakes	equals	1 fresh pepper
1 tablespoon cornstarch	equals	2 tablespoons flour
2 tablespoons egg, powdered	equals	1 egg + 2 tablespoons water
1/2 cup fruit, dried	equals	1 fresh medium-size fruit
1/8 teaspoon garlic powder	equals	1 clove garlic
1/2 teaspoon herbs, dried	equals	1 tablespoon herbs, fresh
2/3 cup honey	equals	1 cup sugar
1/4 cup dried whole milk + 1 cup water	equals	1 cup milk

Measurements

	is equivalent to:
Dash	less than ⅛ teaspoon
3 teaspoons	1 tablespoon
4 tablespoons	¼ cup, or 2 fluid ounces
8 tablespoons	½ cup, or 4 fluid ounces
16 tablespoons	1 cup, or 8 fluid ounces
2 cups	1 pint, or 16 fluid ounces (1 pound)
4 cups	1 quart, or 32 fluid ounces
2 pints	1 quart
4 quarts	1 gallon
16 ounces	1 pound
1 liter	1,000 milliliters
1 liter	1.06 quart
½ liter	1.06 pint
1 gallon of water	8 pounds
1 12-ounce travel mug	1½ cups (if filled to lip)

Calories per Pound of Commonly Used Foods

Breakfast	Calories/pound
Cream of Wheat	1,658
Granola	2,211
Grape-Nuts	1,760
Hash browns—dry	1,600
Oatmeal	1,672
Wheatena	1,618

Dinners	
Bulgur	1,621
Couscous	1,600
Egg noodles	1,760
Falafel	2,200
Lentils	1,860
Macaroni	1,674
Potatoes—sliced	1,624
Potato flakes	1,650

Refried beans	2,200
Rice	1,647
Spaghetti	1,674
Tortillas	1,200

Flour

Bisquick	1,920
Cornmeal	1,610
Muffin mix	2,280
Sweet bread mix	2,000
Wheat	1,651
White	1,650

High-Calorie (High-Fat) Items

Bacon pieces	2,836
Cheddar	1,840
Cream cheese	1,600
Ham	1,800
Margarine	3,200
Mozzarella, real milk	1,280
Oil	4,000
Parmesan	2,080
Peanut butter	2,682
Pepperoni	2,255
Salami	2,041
Smoked salmon	800
Sour cream	1,600
Swiss cheese	1,680
Textured vegetable protein (TVP)	1,500
Tuna, "oil packed"	880
Tuna, "water packed"	720

Trail Food

Apples	1,102
Apricots	1,080
Bagels	1,800
Candy—hard	1,751
Cashews	2,604
Chocolate bars	1,650

Coconut	2,468
Crackers	1,828
Dates	1,243
Fruit bars	3,000
M&Ms	2,100
Mixed nuts	2,694
Peanuts	2,558
Pita bread	1,000
Popcorn	1,642
Power Bars	1,600
Raisins	1,360
Sunflower seeds	2,550
Trail mix	2,000
Walnuts	2,950

Drinks and Sugar

Brown sugar	1,700
Fruit crystals	1,950
Gatorade	1,600
Honey	1,379
Hot chocolate	2,000
Jell-O	1,683
White sugar	1,700

Desserts

Brownie mix	1,828
Cake mix	2,200
Cheesecake mix	3,500
Gingerbread mix	1,928
Pudding	1,637

Miscellaneous

Beef base	1,082
Chicken base	1,117
Corn—dried	1,600
Eggs, powdered	2,697
Instant soups: 1 cup	100
Milk—dried, nonfat	1,625

Peas/carrots—dried	1,200
Peas/onions—dried	1,200
Peppers—dried	1,000
Ramen soup	1,067
Soup mix—veggie	1,600
Tomato base	1,350

Sources of Food and Gear

Note: Most of these products can be ordered from the comfort of the chair in front of your computer.

Just Add Water: Freeze-Dried and Dehydrated Foods

Adventure Food (adventurefood.com)
AlpineAire Foods (alpineaire.com)
Backpacker's Pantry (backpackerspantry.com)
Harmony House Foods (harmonyhousefoods.com)
Harvest Foodworks (harvestfoodworks.com)
Mary Janes Farm (shop.maryjanesfarm.org)
Mountain House (mountainhouse.com)
Richmoor/Natural High (tyry.com)

High-Energy Drinks and Bars

Balance Bar (balance.com)
Clif Bar (clifbar.com)
Emergen-C (emergenc.com)
Gatorade (gatorade.com)
Phix (phix.com)
PowerBar (powerbar.com)
Promax Bar (promaxnutrition.com)
Spark (advocare.com)
Sqwincher (sqwincher.com)

Stoves and Fuel

BioLite (biolitestove.com)
Campingaz (campingaz.com)
Cascade Designs, Inc. (cascadedesigns.com): MSR products.
Coleman Company (coleman.com)
Jetboil (jetboil.com)
Optimus (optimusstoves.com)
Primus (primuscamping.com)

Gear for the Outdoor Kitchen

Backpacker's Pantry (backpackerspantry.com): Evolution cookware
    and more.
BakePacker (bakepacker.com)
Banks Fry-Bake Company (frybake.com): fry-bake pans.
Cascade Designs, Inc. (cascadedesigns.com): MSR.
GSI Outdoors (gsioutdoors.com): lots of stuff.
Leatherman (leatherman.com): multi-tools.
Planetary Design (planetarydesign.us): Bistro French press.
Primus (primuscamping.com): Eta and more.

Water Disinfection

Cascade Designs, Inc. (cascadedesigns.com): SweetWater and MSR.
General Ecology (generalecology.com): First Need.
Katadyn (katadyn.com)

One-Stop Shopping: Everything You Could Possibly Need

Backcountry (backcountry.com)
Backcountry Gear (backcountrygear.com)
Campmor (campmor.com)
CampStuff (campstuff.com)
Eastern Mountain Sports (ems.com)
L.L. Bean (llbean.com)
Recreational Equipment, Inc. (rei.com)

INDEX

ABOUT THE AUTHOR

Buck Tilton has been cooking up meals for bicyclists, paddlers, and backpackers across North and South America. His many books for FalconGuides, including the award-winning *Wilderness First Responder,* have sold more than 100,000 copies combined. He currently lives in Lander, Wyoming.